INFANCY AND CULTURE

T0347473

REFERENCE BOOKS ON FAMILY ISSUES
VOLUME 27
GARLAND REFERENCE LIBRARY OF THE SOCIAL SCIENCES
VOLUME 1168

Infancy and Culture
An International Review and Source Book

Edited by
Hiram E. Fitzgerald
Rosalind B. Johnson
Laurie A. Van Egeren
Domini R. Castellino
Carol Barnes Johnson
Mary Judge-Lawton

Routledge
Taylor & Francis Group

LONDON AND NEW YORK

First published 1999 by Garland Publishing Inc.

Published 2018 by Routledge
2 Park Square, Milton Park, Abingdon, Oxon, OX14 4RN
52 Vanderbilt Avenue, New York, NY 10017

First issued in paperback 2018

Routledge is an imprint of the Taylor & Francis Group, an informa business

Library of Congress Cataloging-in-Publication Data

Infancy and culture : an international review and source book / edited
    by Hiram E. Fitzgerald ... [et al.].
        p.   cm. -- (Reference books on family issues ; v. 27)
(Garland reference library of social science ; v. 1168)
Includes bibliographical references and index.
ISBN 0-8153-2838-9 (alk. paper)
1. Children Cross-cultural studies.   2. Child development Cross
-cultural studies.   3. Child psychology Cross-cultural studies.
I. Fitzgerald, Hiram E.   II. Series.   III. Series: Garland reference
library of social science ; v. 1168.
GN482.I53 1999
305.23--dc21   99-29683
                                                                        CIP

ISBN 13: 978-1-138-99245-0 (pbk)
ISBN 13: 978-0-8153-2838-4 (hbk)

Contents

A Guide to Some Common Acronyms

In order to conserve as much space as possible for citations, we chose to use acronyms for many frequently used assessment tools and other labels used in research with infants. Although this alphabet soup can be annoying, we chose to balance this annoyance against the benefits of including as many citations as possible in the resource book.

BNBAS	Brazelton Neonatal Behavioral Assessment Scale (also, BNAS)
BSID	Bayley Scales of Infant Development
BMI	Bayley Mental Development Index (Scale)
BPI	Bayley Psychomotor Index (Scale)
BW	Birth Weight
CIIS	Catell Infant Intelligence Scales
HHANES-MA	Hispanic Health and Nutrition Examination Survey
HOME	Home Observation for Measurement of the Environment
IBR	Infant Behavior Record
LBW	Low Birth Weight
MLBW	Moderately Low Birth Weight
NICU	Neonatal Intensive Care Unit
SES	Socioeconomic Status
SIDS	Sudden Infant Death Syndrome
WISC-R	Wechsler Intelligence Scale for Children Revised
VLBW	Very Low Birth Weight

Infancy and Culture

1 THE CULTURAL CONTEXT OF INFANCY

Hiram E. Fitzgerald

The idea for this volume was generated in a graduate seminar in developmental psychology that focused on the cultural context of infancy. The seminar was the direct result of several analyses of the published literature that indicated that scientific studies of children of color represented a disproportionately small portion of the publications from several of the most prominent journals in the field of human development. The relative lack of published studies stands in marked contrast to both immigration trends in the United States and the proportion of the United States population that is nonwhite. Since the 1980s nearly 85% of all immigrants to the United States are people of color, from various countries of Asia and the Pacific Rim, South America, the Caribbean, and Mexico. In the year 2000, the population of the United States is projected to be 275 million, a number expected to increase to 383 million by 2050. The white share of the population of 2050 will be close to 50%, a marked reduction from its current 72% of the population market. Because birth statistics are tabulated by the race of the infant's mother, population demographics will underestimate the racial/ethnic diversity of America's population, inasmuch as most mixed-race infants are born to white mothers and nonwhite fathers. Undercounting in the national census has been a more significant problem for population estimates of African Americans, Hispanic Americans, and American Indians, than for Asian Americans and white Americans. Therefore, there are a number of reasons to believe that by 2050, the population of the United States will consist of less than 50% white Americans.

Currently, the United States government compiles statistics on four categories of racial/ethnic "minorities": (1) African Americans or blacks; (2) Asian Americans and Pacific Islanders; (3) American Indians, Eskimos, and Aleuts; and (4) Hispanics. What do such categories mean for the study of infancy? Many authors have drawn attention to the fact that there is rich heterogeneity within each of the government classifications, and that, in fact, there is no classification system that is immune from within- or between-group diversity. Grace (1992) defines blacks as individuals who have cultural ties to Africa, whereas African Americans are defined as black people who are descendants of men and women who were brought to the United States as slaves. She illustrates differences between such groups along the lines of Ogbu's (1998) distinction between voluntary and involuntary immigrants. But even to assign all individuals to a group on the basis of their historical connection to Africa obfuscates the diversity of cultures within Africa itself. In addition, the familial culture of a tenth-generation African American infant may be quite different than that of a first generation infant whose parents immigrated from Cameroon (Bame Nsamenang, 1992). Some investigators contend that because a society's institutions reflect the values, beliefs, and myths of the majority, members of minority groups must either learn their familial culture at home or they may not learn it at all (Wilson, Pina, Chan & Soberanis, 1998).

Hispanic, a term first used by the Bureau of the Census in 1980, refers to individuals residing in the United States whose cultural origins can be traced to Mexico, Puerto Rico, Cuba, Central America, or other Latin American countries. However, there are various meanings of the term "Hispanic" and extraordinary diversity among the countries and cultures it is claimed to represent (Olvera et al., 1998). As Klor de Alva (1988) notes: "Different Hispanic groups, generally concentrated in different regions of the country have little knowledge of each other and are often as surprised as non-Hispanics to discover the cultural gulfs that separate them" (107).

Similarly, the term "Asian/Pacific Islander" refers to more than 60 separate ethnic/racial groups and subgroups (Coll & Magnuson, 1998; Kim, McLeon & Shantzis, 1992), and all of this pales to the heterogeneity found in 512 federally recognized Native entities and 365 state-recognized Indian tribes. And all of these groups must fit into the collective study of human infancy in order to elaborate fully the diverse contexts within which infants and their caregivers engage in the process of development. The demand to better understand individual differences and to be sensitive to the rich diversity that may exist within a culture, however, should not blind investigators to the study of similarities among groups. McAdoo (1998) notes that studies of families of color may reveal many commonalities in family coping strategies, as for example, may relate to family resilience. Such commonalities may be informative about how minority families buffer the pervasive challenges of the dominant culture with respect to the values, codes, and behaviors expected of individuals residing in that culture (Althen, 1988).

Kim and Choi (1994) divide countries on two dimensions, individualism and consciousness. Countries emphasizing high individualism (United States, Australia, Canada, Netherlands, New Zealand) and those emphasizing high collectivism (Venezuela, Colombia, Pakistan, Peru, Taiwan, Thailand, Hong Kong, Korea) may have more within-category commonality than between-category commonality. Moreover, it may be that countries with higher degrees of collectivism have families more deeply committed to stability, than do countries that place great emphasis on individualism. If so, one might expect greater resilience among children whose culture supports such values as emotional dependence, group solidarity, sharing, duties to obligations, and group decision process, in contrast to autonomy, privacy, emotional independence, pleasure seeking, and financial security (Kim & Choi, 1994). The key point is that cultural contrasts do not necessarily lead only to identification of differences, and in fact, the identification of similarities may represent a more constructive approach to cultural competence.

It seems abundantly clear that through the next century America will become a predominantly nonwhite population of extraordinary diversity, perhaps unparalleled in human history. Yet, we know very little about such diversity. One might expect that a culture purporting to be a melting pot would have produced a diverse scientific literature on human development, appropriate to the heterogeneity of its population. But this has not been the case. McLoyd and Randolph (1985) scanned published articles in the journal *Child Development* and reported a low percentage of studies of African Americans, with the exception of a short-lived increase during the 1970s. Graham's (1992) analysis of 6 journals published by the American Psychological Association provides additional evidence of a decrease in the number and percentage of articles focused on studies of African Americans from 1970 to 1989. A follow-up analysis of *Child Development* (Spencer & McLoyd, 1990) reported maintenance of a low percentage of publications involving African Americans through the 1980s, a finding confirmed by Hagen and Conley (1994). In addition, several reviewers identified similarly low rates of published articles that involved participants who were Asian American or Hispanic. And studies of Native Americans are practically nonexistent.

A preliminary analysis of articles published in the *Infant Mental Health Journal* (Fitzgerald, 1997) is consistent with those noted above, a disproportionately low number of published articles involving infants of color and/or infants residing outside of the United States. Because the "browning of America" will take place more rapidly at the youngest age levels (de Leon Siantz, 1998), the lack of scientific knowledge about the early years of life among nonwhite infants means that practitioners cannot be fully informed about the significance of cultural variability apropos of preventive-intervention programs directed at the birth to age five population. Because this age group is the one with the highest percentage of children living in poverty, with its correlated social and educational difficulties, it is especially at risk for development of problem behavior. The rich variety of early intervention programs targeting the birth to age five population, such as Early Head Start and Head Start, reflect societal awareness that much must be done to alter the developmental course for many of these children. Societal awareness, however, does not always translate into minority culture awareness, because societal awareness is so strongly embedded in the mores, values, and beliefs of the dominant group.

In 1964, Yvonne Brackbill and her associates published a cross-tabulated bibliography of 1,733 studies of the human infant dating from the late 1800s to 1963. Of the total number of citations in her volume, 24% involved infants of color and/or infants living outside of the United States. Only slightly more than 1% could be classified in the U.S. Census Bureau contemporary definitions of "minorities." Twenty-two percent involved infants reared outside of the United States. However, as Table 1 indicates, the majority of these studies did not involve infants of color.

This, then, was the background for the seminar. Although analyses of the published literature uniformly pointed to the low incidence of infants of color as research participants, such analysis involved relatively few of the possible scientific journals that may contain articles involving infants of color. Members of the seminar, all of whom are coeditors of the volume, decided to approach the literature search from a different perspective. All major data bases of published scientific literature were scanned for studies of infants, with the provisos that (1) an English-language abstract must be available; (2) that the content of the study must be behavioral, or predominately behavioral; (3) the race/ethnicity/nationality of the infants is reported; and (4) the study must have been published between 1970 and 1997. We most likely underestimated the number of citations. Authors may not have provided the details we needed in order to classify the infants as to their race/ethnicity/nationality. Studies of genetic and/or chromosomal anomalies were not included unless behavioral outcomes were reported. Studies that were predominately biological or medical were not included, unless, of course, behavioral outcomes were a key part of the study. And, finally, we did not include abstracts for journals published in languages other than English.

Our goal was to assemble a resource that included more than just the studies of infants of color in American culture. Therefore, all studies were

Table 1 Racial/Ethnic and International Analysis of Citations in
Brackbill's (1964) Cross-Indexed Bibliography of
Infant Studies (1,733 citations)

Race/ Ethnicity	Number of Citations	Percent of Total
African American	10	<1
Asian American	9	<1
American Indian	3	<1

Nationality	Number of Citations	Percent of Total	Nationality	Number of Citations	Percent of Total
German	89	5	Chinese	3	<1
Soviet*	70	4	Indian	3	<1
French	59	3.5	Iranian	3	<1
British	50	3	Polish	3	<1
Canadian	27	1.5	Scot	3	<1
African	13	<1	Israeli	2	<1
Swiss	13	<1	Swedish	2	<1
Czech*	6	<1	Australian	1	<1
Italian	5	<1	Jamaican	1	<1
Austrian	4	<1	Ukranian	1	<1
Dutch**	4	<1	Unclassified	28	1.5
Japanese	4	<1			

* Since 1964 geopolitical regions have changed. The Soviet Union included what are now a variety of independent countries, although most of the research involving infants was conducted in what is now Russia. Most of the studies listed under "Czech" were conducted in Prague, at the Institute for Mother and Child under the direction of Hanus Papousek, so they were classified as Czech rather than Slovak.
** The Netherlands

classified as a function of where the infants resided so that there is an infant of color-by-culture interaction for all citations in the volume, even for cultures where the dominant racial/ethnic population is nonwhite. Our search through 175 journals led us to 118 (see Appendix A, p. 12) that contained articles meeting the inclusion criteria, and these journals yielded 386 articles that were abstracted for inclusion in this volume. All abstracts were severely edited or completely rewritten, a list of 10 key words was generated for each article, and indexing decisions were based on group consensus as to the major findings reflected by the article. The indexed key words refer to the topics covered in each article and may or may not be reflected in the brief abstracts provided in this volume. We did not evaluate the quality of the published work; we accepted at face value that published articles survived the peer review process. Once classified into geographic region and alphabetized within region, the articles were numbered consecutively. Therefore, when searching for articles on a particular topic, keep in mind that the items in the subject index refer to the numbers of specific articles, not to page numbers in the book. For example, "cradling, 329, 330" indicates that cradling is a key topic in both citations 329 and 330. Exactly the same approach applies to the author index. So, "Fitzgerald, 33, 54, 55, 127" refers to the four articles in which Fitzgerald was an author. The italicized numbers that appear in the introductory text prior to each unit refer to citations that are listed in the unit and in the subject and author indexes.

Brackbill's (1964) volume was intended to serve as a catalyst for what then was the emergent field of infancy. The 1960s was an exciting time for the study of infancy. Formal laboratories were established at Brown University (Lewis Lipsitt), Yale University (William Kessen), the University of Denver (Yvonne Brackbill), University of North Carolina (Harriet Reingold), Fels Research Institute (Jerome Kagan), Case Western Reserve University (Robert Fantz), and the University of Wisconsin (Frances Graham), among others, and soon replications of these laboratories appeared throughout the country, established by students who were attracted to these laboratories for their doctoral studies. In addition, the 1960s was a decade of discovery, not only of the extraordinary competencies of the infant (Stone, Smith & Murphy, 1973), but also of markedly different ways of thinking about infancy and early development (Piaget, 1952). Basic research focusing on the first three years of life helped to provide convincing evidence that behaviorist explanations of development were inadequate to account for the extraordinary organizations and reorganizations that mark early development. Despite the fact that infants from other cultures played a key role in structuring this new view (Ainsworth, 1967; Bowlby, 1969; Piaget, 1952), cultural context was not framed as a key determinant of individual differences. Investigators were driven by theories that focused on species (and, presumably, heritable) characteristics, not on individual differences or person-environment transactions. With respect to socialization of the child, the quality of the mother-infant relationship overshadowed issues related to the importance of supplemental caregivers or to the context of caregiving (Greenfield & Cocking, 1998).

During the past decade, investigators have focused increasing attention to filling in the knowledge gap, and numerous edited and authored books have been published on cultural competence. A list of some of these volumes is provided at the end of this chapter in a section titled "General Resources for Literature on Children and Families of Color."

We hope that this volume broadens the research agenda in several distinct ways. First, study of human infancy needs to expand across a broad range of cultures, and such study must not be confined to an occasional investigation. The occasional oftentimes becomes the standard in the literature obfuscating within culture variability. One study of the father's role in childbirth, for example, may accurately describe paternal behavior in the urban setting, but may be at odds with paternal behavior in rural settings. One study of attachment behavior may identify between-culture differences in the number of infants assigned to the securely attached category, but fail to provide an in-depth understanding of within-culture variability. This leads to the second goal of the volume: to highlight the need for in-depth study of within-culture variability, using both quantitative and qualitative scientific methods. We hope that this compilation entices journal editors and reviewers to consider inclusion of more descriptive studies of development during the early years of life so that a more complete picture of *human* development evolves. It is a truism that most of the world's infants are not white, many if not most live in poor socioeconomic conditions, and many live in families that are not organized as traditional nuclear units (Loukas et al., 1998). In short, we do not know enough about the varieties of human experience. Finally, greater specification of the impact of culture in shaping affective, cognitive, and interpersonal behavior during the early years of life will enhance our understanding of the dynamic interplay between developmentally stable species characteristics and developmentally labile population characteristics. This is simply another way of characterizing the transactional relationship between nature (biology) and nurture (experience) with respect to understanding the processes that regulate the systemic organization of human behavior (Ford & Lerner, 1992; Miller & Miller, 1992; von Bertalanffy, 1968).

REFERENCES

Ainsworth, M.D.S. (1967). *Infancy in Uganda: Infant care and the growth of attachment.* Baltimore: Johns Hopkins Press.

Althen, G. (1988). *American ways: A guide for foreigners in the United States.* Yarmouth, MA: Intercultural Press.

Bame Nsamenang, A. (1992). *Human development in cultural context: A third world perspective.* Newbury Park, CA: Sage.

Bowlby, J. (1969). *Attachment and loss, volume one: Attachment.* New York: Basic Books.

Brackbill, Y. (Ed.). (1964). *Research in infant behavior: A cross-indexed bibliography.* Baltimore: Williams and Wilkins.

Coll, C.G., & Magnuson, K. (1998). Theory and research with children of color: Implications for social policy. In H.E. Fitzgerald, B.M. Lester, & B.S. Zuckerman (Eds). *Children of color: Research, health, and policy issues.* (pp. 219–256). New York: Garland.

de Leon Siantz, M.L. (1998). The mental health status of Hispanic immigrant children. In H.E. Fitzgerald, B.M. Lester & B.S. Zuckerman (Eds). *Children of color: Research, health, and policy issues.* (pp. 95–120). New York: Garland.

Fitzgerald, H.E. (1997). Infant mental health: An interdisciplinary and international perspective for families with infants and toddlers. *South African Journal of Child and Adolescent Psychiatry, 9,* 168–172.

Fitzgerald, H.E., Lester, B.M., & Zuckerman, B.S. (Eds). (1996). *Children of poverty: Research, health, and policy issues.* New York: Garland.

Fitzgerald, H.E., Lester, B.M., & Zuckerman, B.S. (Eds.). (1998). *Children of color: Research, health, and policy issues.* New York: Garland.

Ford, D.H., & Lerner, R.M. (1992). *Developmental systems theory: An integrative approach.* Newbury Park, CA: Sage.

Grace, C.A. (1992). Practical considerations for program professionals and evaluators working with African American communities. In M.A. Orlandi, R. Weston, & L.G. Epstein (Eds.). *Cultural competence for evaluators* (pp. 55–74). Rockville, MD: U.S. Office of Substance Abuse Prevention.

Graham, S. (1992). "Most of the subjects were white and middle class." Trends in published research on African Americans in selected American Psychological Association journals, 1970–1989. *American Psychologist, 47,* 629–639.

Greenfield, P.M., & Cocking, R.R. (Eds.). *Cross-cultural roots of minority child development.* Hillsdale, NJ: Erlbaum.

Hagen, J.W., & Conley, A.C. (1994, Spring). Ethnicity and race of children studied in *Child Development,* 1980–1993. *Society for Research in Child Development Newsletter, 6–7.*

Huston, A. (Ed.). (1991). *Children in poverty: Child development and public policy.* New York: Cambridge University Press.

Kagitçiba«i, C. (1996). *Family and human development across cultures: A view from the other side.* Mahwah, NJ: Erlbaum.

Kim, U. & Choi, S-H. (1994). Individualism, collectivism, and child development: A Korean perspective. In P.M. Greenfield & R.R. Cocking (Eds.). *Cross-cultural roots of minority child development.* (pp. 227–257). Hillsdale, NJ: Erlbaum.

Kim, S., McLeon, J.H., & Shantzis, C. (1992). Cultural competence for evaluators working with Asian American communities: Some practical considerations. In M.A. Orlandi, R. Weston, & L.G. Epstein (Eds.). *Cultural competence for evaluators* (pp. 55–74). Rockville, MD: U.S. Office of Substance Abuse Prevention.

Klor de Alva, J.J. (1988). Telling Hispanics apart: Latin sociocultural diversity. In E. Acosta-Belen & B.R. Sjostrom (Eds.). *The Hispanic experience in the United States* (pp. 107–136). New York: Praeger.

Lamb, M.E. (Ed.). (1987). *The father's role: Cross-cultural perspectives.* Hillsdale, NJ: Erlbaum.

Lamb, M.E., & Keller, H. (Eds.). (1991). *Infant development: Perspectives from German-speaking countries.* Hillsdale, NJ: Erlbaum

Loukas, A., Twitchell, G.R., Piejak, L.A., Fitzgerald, H.E., & Zucker, R.A. (1998). The family as a unity of interacting personalities. In L. L'Abate (Ed.). *Handbook of family psychopathology.* (pp. 35–59). New York: Guilford.

McAdoo, H.P. (1998). Diverse children of color: Research and policy. In H.E. Fitzgerald, B.M. Lester, & B.S. Zuckerman (Eds). *Children of color: Research, health, and policy issues.* (pp. 205–218). New York: Garland.

McLoyd, V.C. (1998). Conceptual and methodological issues in the study of ethnic minority children and adolescents. In H.E. Fitzgerald, B.M. Lester, & B.S.

Zuckerman (Eds). *Children of color: Research, health, and policy issues.* (pp. 3–24). New York: Garland.

McLoyd, V.C., & Randolph, S. (1985). Secular trends in the study of Afro-American children: A review of *Child Development*, 1936–1980. In A. Smuts & J. Hagen (Eds.). History and research in child development. *Monographs of the Society for Research in Child Development. 50* (4–5, Serial No. 211), 78–92.

Miller, J.G., & Miller, J.L. (1992). Cybernetics, general systems theory, and living systems theory. In R.L. Levine & H.E. Fitzgerald (Eds.). *Analysis of dynamic psychological systems, Volume 1: Basic approaches to general systems, dynamic systems, and cybernetics* (pp. 9–34). New York: Plenum.

Nugent, J.K., Lester, B.M., & Brazelton, T.B. (Eds.). (1989). *The cultural context of infancy, volume one: Biology, culture, and infant development.* Norwood, NJ: Ablex.

Nugent, J.K., Lester, B.M., & Brazelton, T.B. (Eds.) (1991). *The cultural context of infancy, volume two: Multicultural and interdisciplinary approaches to parent-infant relations.* Norwood, NJ: Ablex.

Ogbu, J.U. (1994). From cultural differences to differences in cultural frame of reference. In P.M. Greenfield & R.R. Cocking (Eds.). *Cross-cultural roots of minority child development.* (pp. 365–392). Hillsdale, NJ: Erlbaum.

Ogbu, J.U. (1998). Cultural context of children's development. In H.E. Fitzgerald, B.M. Lester, & B.S. Zuckerman (Eds.). *Children of color: Research, health, and policy issues.* New York: Garland.

Olvera, N., Hays, J.H., Power, T.G., & Yañez, C. (1998). Health behaviors of Mexican American families. In H.E. Fitzgerald, B.M. Lester, & B.S. Zuckerman (Eds). *Children of color: Research, health, and policy issues.* (pp. 121–140). New York: Garland

Piaget, J. (1952). *The origin's of intelligence in children.* New York: International Universities Press.

Slonim, M.B. (1991). *Children, culture, and ethnicity: Evaluating and understanding the impact.* New York: Garland.

Spencer, M.B., & McLoyd, V.C. (1990). Special issue on minority children. *Child Development, 61.*

Stone, Smith, & Murphy (Eds.). (1973). *The competent infant.* New York: Basic Books.

von Bertalanffy, L. (1968). *General systems theory.* New York: Braziller.

Wilson, M.H., Pina, L.M., Chan, R.W., & Soberanis, D.D. (1998). Ethnic minority families and the majority education system. In H.E. Fitzgerald, B.M. Lester, & B.S. Zuckerman (Eds). *Children of color: Research, health, and policy issues.* (pp. 257–280). New York: Garland.

GENERAL RESOURCES FOR LITERATURE ON CHILDREN AND FAMILIES OF COLOR

Brislin, R.W. (Ed.). (1990). *Applied cross cultural psychology.* Newbury Park, CA: Sage.

Burlew, A.K.H., Banks, W.C., McAdoo, H.P., & Ajani ya Azibo, D. (Eds.). (1992). *African American psychology: Theory research and practice.* Newbury Park, CA: Sage.

Carrasquillo, A.L. (1991). *Hispanic children and youth in the United States.* New York: Garland.

Field, T.M., Sostek, A.M., Vietze, P., & Leiderman, P.H. (Eds.). (1981). *Culture and early interactions.* Hillsdale, NJ: Erlbaum.

Jackson, J.S., Chatters, L.M., & Taylor, R.J. (Eds.). (1993). *Aging in black America.* Newbury Park, CA: Sage.

Johnson-Powell, G., & Yamamoto, J. (Eds). (1997). *Transcultural child development: Psychological assessment and treatment.* New York: Wiley.

Kamhi, A.G., Pollock, K.E., & Harris, J.L. (Eds.). (1996). *Communication development and disorders in African American children.* Baltimore: Paul H. Brookes.

Leiderman, P.H., Tulkin, S.R., & Rosenfeld, A. (Eds). (1977). *Culture and infancy: Variations in the human experience.* New York: Academic Press.

Lynch, E.W., & Hanson, M.J. (Eds.). (1992). *Developing cross cultural competence: A guide for working with young children and their families.* Baltimore: Paul H. Brookes.

McAdoo, H.P. (Ed.). (1993). *Family ethnicity.* Newbury Park, CA: Sage.

Padilla, A.M. (Ed.). (1995). *Hispanic psychology: Critical issues in theory and research.* Thousand Oaks, CA: Sage.

Phinney, J.S., & Rotheram, M.J. (Eds.). (1987). *Children's ethnic socialization.* Newbury Park, CA: Sage.

Trevathan, W.R. (1987). *Human birth: An evolutionary perspective.* New York: Aldine de Gruyter.

Appendix A

Journals Searched

Acta Paedologica
Adolescence
Advances in Alcohol & Substance Abuse
Alcoholism: Clinical & Experimental Research
American Anthropologist
American Indian & Alaska Native Mental Health Research
American Journal of Clinical Nutrition
American Journal of Community Psychology
American Journal of Diseases of Children
American Journal of Drug & Alcohol Abuse
American Journal of Epidemiology
American Journal of Mental Deficiency
American Journal of Obstetrics and Gynecology
American Journal of Orthopsychiatry
American Journal of Perinatology
American Journal of Preventive Medicine
American Journal of Psychiatry
American Journal of Public Health
American Journal of Social Psychiatry
Annals of the New York Academy of Sciences
Annual Progress in Child Psychiatry & Child Development
Annual Review of Medicine
Applied Psychology: An International Review
Archives of Disease in Childhood: Fetal and Neonatal Edition
Archives of the Diseases of Childhood
Archives of French Pediatrics
Archives of Pediatrics and Adolescent Medicine
ASDC Journal of Dentistry for Children
Association of Black Nursing Faculty in Higher Education Journal
Australian & New Zealand Journal of Psychiatry
Australian and New Zealand Journal of Sociology
Black Sociologist
Boletin de Psicologia (Cuba)
British Medical Journal
Bulletin of the Pan American Health Organization
Canadian Journal of African Studies
Canadian Journal of Public Health
Canadian Journal of Sport Sciences

Canadian Medical Association Journal
Child Abuse and Neglect
Child Care, Health and Development
Child Development
Child Psychiatry & Human Development
Children's Health Care
Collegium Antropologicum
Current Anthropology
Current Opinion in Obstetrics and Gynecology
Developmental Medicine & Child Neurology
Developmental Psychobiology
Developmental Psychology
Early Child Development & Care
Early Childhood Research Quarterly
Early Human Development
Educational & Psychological Measurement
Ethnicity and Disease
Ethology and Sociobiology
Ethos
Evaluation Quarterly
Exceptional Children
Growth
Health Care for Women International
Health Education Quarterly
Hispanic Journal of Behavioral Sciences
Human Biology
Human Development
Human Organization
Indian Journal of Medical Research
Indian Journal of Pediatrics
Infant Behavior & Development
Infant Mental Health Journal
Infant-Toddler Intervention: The Transdisciplinary Journal
International Family Planning Perspectives
International Journal of Behavioral Development
International Journal of Epidemiology
International Journal of Gynaecology and Obstetrics
International Journal of Nursing Studies
International Journal of Psychology
Journal of Abnormal Psychology
Journal of Adolescence
Journal of Adolescent Health
Journal of Adolescent Health Care
Journal of Adolescent Research
Journal of the American Academy of Child and Adolescent Psychiatry
Journal of the American Dietary Association
Journal of the American Medical Association
Journal of the American Medical Women's Association
Journal of Anthropological Research
Journal of Applied Developmental Psychology
Journal of Biosocial Science
Journal of Black Psychology
Journal of Child Language
Journal of Child Psychology and Psychiatry and Allied Disciplines
Journal of Clinical Child Psychology
Journal of Clinical Epidemiology

Journal of Communication
Journal of Community Psychology
Journal of Comparative Family Studies
Journal of Cross-Cultural Psychology
Journal of Developing Areas
Journal of Developmental & Behavioral Pediatrics
Journal of Early Intervention
Journal of Epidemiology & Community Health
Journal of Family History
Journal of Family Issues
Journal of Family Practice
Journal of Genetic Psychology
Journal of Health, Politics, Policy and Law
Journal of Health & Social Behavior
Journal of Health and Social Policy
Journal of Human Movement Studies
Journal of Marriage and the Family
Journal of the Medical Association of Georgia
Journal of National Black Nurses' Association
Journal of the National Medical Association
Journal of Obstetric and Gynaecology of the British Commonwealth
Journal of Obstetric, Gynecologic, and Neonatal Nursing
Journal of Pediatrics
Journal of Perinatal and Neonatal Nursing
Journal of Perinatology
Journal of Psychology
Journal of Public Health Policy
Journal of Reproductive and Infant Psychology
Journal of Research on Adolescence
Journal of the Singapore Paediatric Society
Journal of Social Behavior & Personality
Journal of Speech & Hearing Research
Journal of Substance Abuse
Journal of Tropical Pediatrics
Language in Society
Leisure Studies
Maternal Child Nursing Journal
Merrill Palmer Quarterly
Neurobehavioral Toxicology & Teratology
Neurotoxicology & Teratology
New England Journal of Medicine
New Zealand Medical Journal
Obesity Research
Obstetrics and Gynecology
Paediatric Perinatal Epidemiology
Pediatrics
Perceptual & Motor Skills
Phylon
Physical & Occupational Therapy in Pediatrics
Physiology Behavior
Population
Population and Development Review
Population Studies
Pre- & Peri-Natal Psychology Journal
Psychiatry

Psychology and Developing Societies
Public Health Nursing
Public Health Reports
Reading Teacher
Rural Sociology
Salud Publica de Mexico
Sex Roles
Singapore Medical Journal
Sleep
Social Biology
Social Development
Social Forces
Social Science Journal
Social Science & Medicine
Social Science Quarterly
Social Work in Education
Sociology and Social Research
South African Journal of Physiotherapy
South African Journal of Psychology
South African Medical Journal
Southern Medical Journal
Studies in Family Planning
Texas Medicine
Topics in Early Childhood Special Education
Voprosy-Pitaniia
Western Journal of Nursing Research

PART 1
NORTH AMERICA

2 RESEARCH ON INFANTS OF AFRICAN DESCENT IN NORTH AMERICA AND THE CARIBBEAN

FROM HISTORICAL DEPRIVATION TO NEW QUESTIONS OF RESILIENCY

Rosalind B. Johnson

The people of African decent in North America and the Caribbean have diverse traditions and values. This group of people includes African Americans, African Canadians, Haitians, Jamaicans, and Puerto Ricans,[1] among others. However, the present literature does not reflect this diversity. Though the term black is widely used throughout the world to describe people of African descent, this term does not capture the rich ethnic backgrounds and cultural diversity of the people (Slomin, 1991). The black people in North America and the Caribbean have created an abundance of variation in terms of traditions and values.

"Black" is used to encompass the many subgroups of black North American and Caribbean people. Even though these subgroups share a common African heritage, differences among them result from the environmental experiences they have encountered (Slonim, 1991). There are some traditional characteristics shared by black people that provide a general frame of reference for understanding black children and their families. However, African Americans and Caribbean blacks have different family structures, child-rearing practices, religions, values, languages, health care systems, and educational systems. Caribbean blacks share a similar heritage with African Americans. However, because of circumstances of history and environment, Caribbean blacks represent distinctive cultural subgroups quite different from American blacks. These differences are a reflection of the European cultures that immigrated to the Caribbean—British, French, Spanish, and Dutch (Slonim, 1991).

There are black families of all socioeconomic levels, beliefs, values, and cultures, and thus there is no such entity as a typical black family (Slonim, 1991). The diversity that exists among black families is rooted in variation of geographic residence, family values, socioeconomic status, and religious background. The effects of poverty and racism also contribute to the wide variation that exists among black families.

Even though blacks in the United States comprise an estimated 12% of the population, the infancy literature does not reflect this proportion. Moreover, black infants in Canada and the Caribbean have been virtually ignored by researchers. This lack of research on black Canadians and Caribbeans is surprising given the geographical nearness to the United States and the economical and political ties that link these countries and territories.

CURRENT LITERATURE

The current review identified 188 articles that were published on black infants between 1970 and 1997. All of these studies were conducted in the United States. Several publications track first- and second-generation immigrants from the Caribbean in the United States (de Cubas & Field, 1984, 45). Nevertheless few research articles are published that originate in Canada or Caribbean countries and/or territories. Beyond the sparse research on black infant development in Canada and the Caribbean, the infancy articles published in the United States have had a very narrow focus on at-risk and low-income populations (Rosser & Randolph, 1989).

Even though more blacks are better off economically and educationally than 30 years ago, the infancy literature does not reflect this progress. Seventy-four percent of the studies focus on at-risk populations, such as low-income, low birth weight, prenatal drug exposure, prematurity, and adolescent parenthood (Adams, Campbell & Ramey, 1984, 1; Barclay, 1985, 11; Roth et al., 1995, 149; Schoendorf & Kiely, 1992, 156; Slesinger, 1980, 163; Stark, 1982, 165; Taylor, Katz & Moos, 1995, 175). In addition, this literature focuses on studies contrasting blacks and other subgroups (Berlin et al., 1995, 13; Bertoli, Rent & Rent, 1984, 14; Coll, Spekoski & Lester, 1981, 40; Collins & David, 1992, 42; Dowling & Fisher, 1987, 46; Hanline, 1992, 74).

Of the six studies that included black fathers and infants, four focused on both mothers and fathers. The studies investigating fathers focus on child care issues and transition to parenthood (Bradley, 1984, 24; Hobbs & Wimbish, 1977, 80; Hossain & Roopnarine, 1994, 83; Hossain, 1993, 82; Yogman, Kindlon & Earls, 1995, 186). For example, Hossain (1993, 82) found that traditional gender-differentiated patterns of involvement in care giving and household work existed among dual-earner African American families with infants. In addition, Hossain and Roopnarine (1994, 83) found that African American fathers were more likely to play with their infants than to feed or clean them.

Because less than 4% of the studies included fathers there is a need for future research in the area of black fatherhood. However, the exclusion of fathers in infant research seems to be consistent across all ethnic groups. The literature documents what a father-absent black family is like, but there is limited research focusing on what a father-present black family is like. Thus, more studies are needed that focus on two-parent black families, irrespective of the father's social or biological status.

The alleviation of economic, educational, health, and political difficulties faced by black people has been a primary focus of several intervention programs and policies across the United States. Several researchers have focused on determining the impact of such programs and policies on black infant development (Butler, 1992, 32). Numerous studies examined the impact of health care intervention on infant mortality rates (Davis, 1988, 44; Druschel et al., 1989, 47; Emanuel, Hale & Berg, 1989, 49; Ferguson & Myers, 1990, 52; Goldenberg et al., 1996, 68; Hale & Druschel, 1989, 73; Hummer, 1993, 87; Johnston & Beller, 1976, 98; Jones, Stockwell & Wicks, 1982, 100; Kempe et al., 1992, 102; Kovar, 1977, 110; Powell-Griner, 1988, 141; Reeb et al., 1987, 146). For example, Alo, Howe, and Nelson (1993, 6) found that low birthweight and premature birth of black infants in Illinois contributed to the higher mortality rates for these infants. Furthermore, other investigators report that the very low birthweight rate for black infants is more than three times greater than white infants (Berg et al., 1994, 12).

The literature suggests that although the mortality rates for black infants have decreased over the years, they are still higher than mortality rates for white infants (Kerr, Ying & Spears, 1995, 104). The low birthweights for blacks follow the same pattern for infant mortality rates. Some studies show marked improvements in the birthweight of black infants (Bertoli, Rent & Rent, 1984, 14; Bulter, 1992, 32). Better prenatal care and maternal demographics (e.g., educational attainment, marital status, and income level) contribute to this improvement (Atrash, Rowley & Hogue, 1992, 9; Harris, Roland & McBarnett, 1990, 78; Rowley, 1994, 150).

Black infant studies have focused on low-income populations. More than half of the studies reviewed in this chapter involve low-income samples. This literature focuses on descriptions of demographic and socioeconomic risk factors that challenge infant development. These demographic and socioeconomic factors include maternal education, maternal age, and martial status. For example, Bertoli, Rent, and Rent (1984, 14) found that the strongest predictor of infant mortality was maternal education. In general, mothers of premature and low birthweight infants are poorly educated, have low incomes, and unplanned pregnancies (Boone, 1982, 20; 1985, 21). However, black mothers are more likely to have premature and low birthweight infants when compared to white mothers regardless of educational and/or income level (Hulsey et al. 1991; *86;* Kleinman & Kessel, 1987, *107).* Causes for such differences have yet to be identified.

Several studies examine cognitive development (King & Seegmiller, 1973, *106;* Liaw & Brooks-Gunn, 1993, *120),* language development (Blake, 1993, *19;* Robert et al., *1995, 147),* mother-infant interaction (Field et al., 1980, *54;* Field, 1981, *59;* Field, 1990, *57;* Ramey, Farran & Campbell, 1979, *142;* Stevens & Duffield, 1986, *168),* motor development (Malina, 1988, *124),* temperament (Contreras, 1995, *43;* Gennaro, Tulman & Fawcett, 1990, *65),* and visual habituation of black infants (Johnson & Brody, 1977, *99).* The quality of the home environment is of special interest for studies of cognitive development and mother-infant interaction (Bradley & Caldwell, 1981, *23;* Bradley, 1984, *24;* Bradley, et al. 1995, *26;* King, 1982, *105).*

Anderson-Yockel (1994, *8)* observed communication styles between black mother-infant dyads during three book-reading activities. It was concluded that African American mothers used significantly fewer questioning behaviors and their children produced more spontaneous verbalizations when compared to white mother-infant dyads. Broussard (1995, *29)* failed to demonstrate secure attachment between adolescent mothers and their newborns. Several other studies compared gross motor milestones between black and white infants (Allen & Alexander, 1990, *5;* Carlson et al., 1986, *35;* Cintas, 1988, *36),* and Capute et al. (1985, *34)* found that black infants attained motor milestones earlier than white infants.

The study of prenatal drug and alcohol exposure comprises a significant portion of the citations listed in this section (Lanehart et al., 1994, *113;* Marcus, Hans & Jeremy, 1983, *126;* Marcus et al., 1984, *127;* Sagatun-Edwards, Saylor & Shifflett, 1995, *152;* Harsham, Keller & Disbrow, 1994, *79;* Jacobson et al., 1992, *93;* Jacobson et al., 1993, *94;* Jacobson, Jacobson & Sokol, 1994, *96;* Singleton, Harrell & Kelly, 1986, *162;* Smith et al., 1986, *164;* Ward et al., 1990, *180).* Unborn infants are vulnerable to the effects of alcohol and drugs injested by their mothers. The effects seem to be greater for infants whose mothers are poorly educated, have poor nutrition and low-income levels (Coles et al., 1992, *39).* Coles et al. (1985, *37)* found that neonates exposed to alcohol during gestation displayed significant alterations in reflexive behavior, less mature motor behavior, and higher activity level in comparison to unexposed infants. Coles, Smith and Falek (1987, *38)* also found similar effects for infants exposed to alcohol during gestation.

LIMITATIONS OF CURRENT LITERATURE

There are several shortcomings of the present black infancy literature. First,

Canadian and Caribbean blacks have been virtually ignored by researchers. Second, about 75% of the articles in this chapter focus on at-risk and low-income populations. Noticeably absent are studies focusing on normative black infant development across the full range of socioeconomic classes. Equally absent are studies focusing on the cultural context of infant development throughout the countries of North America, including the Caribbean.

Even though there is a strong tradition of the role of extended families in child-rearing practices (Wilson, 1990, *183*), very few studies address this issue. Flaherty (1988, *61*) found that the mothers of adolescent mothers helped the family to cope with a new baby by managing resources. The type of discipline for black children also receives limited attention from researchers (Slonim, 1991).

It is evident through past research that value is added to the field of infancy study through inclusion of all infants (Slonim, 1991). In addition to strengthening the field of infant studies, an increase in the knowledge of ethnic diversity in infancy development can better inform social and public policy. As the population of black, Asian, and Latino infants continues to grow in the United States and across the world, it is essential to expand our knowledge of infant development to more accurately describe the range of variation across cultural contexts.

Future Directions in Literature

Moving from a deficit approach for studying black infants to an asset approach will fundamentally change the content base of our knowledge of infant development as well as the nature of the questions asked. Historically, blacks have been viewed as disadvantaged people and research on their infants has reflected this perspective (Rosser & Randolph, 1989). As perspectives on black people change, so will the issues that define the research agenda. These changes will not occur immediately. However, as more researchers acknowledge the need to change the theories and methods that drive the research on black infants, they will force a paradigmatic reorientation that will influence all studies of human infancy and build stronger ties among the various disciplines that are concerned with human development (Burlew et al., 1992; Rosser & Randolph, 1989; Slonim, 1991).

Future research in this area should focus on a variety of areas:

- within ethnic variation among black infants
- longitudinal studies of black infant development
- normative samples of black infants
- black infants of two-parent families

- child-rearing practices
- black infants across socioeconomic classes
- black fathers
- studies attending to the blacks infants of all North American and Caribbean countries

Overall, the research available to researchers of black infants has been limited by the theories and methods that drive this research. However, as researchers reorientate the paradigm of this field, a rich and countless set of new research questions will emerge about black infant development.

NOTE

1. Puerto Rican infant studies will be discussed with Latino infant studies in Chapter 4.

REFERENCES

Burlew, A.K.H., Banks, W.C., McAdoo, H.P., & Azibo, D.A. (Eds.). (1992). *African American psychology: Theory, research and practice* (pp. 1–3). Newbury Park: Sage.
Rosser, P.L., & Randolph, S.M. (1989). Black American infants: The Howard University normative study. In J.K. Nugent, B.M. Lester, & T.B. Brazelton (Eds.). *The cultural context of infancy, volume one: Biology, culture, and infant development* (pp. 133–165). Norwood, NJ: Ablex.
Slonim, M.B. (1991). *Children, culture, and ethnicity: Evaluating and understanding the impact* (pp. 195–207). New York: Garland.

RESOURCES

1. Adams, J.L., Campbell, F.A., & Ramey, C.T. (1984). Infants' home environments: A study of screening efficiency. *American Journal of Mental Deficiency, 89,* 133–139.
    The predictive ability of the HOME was assessed for black infants from low-income families at risk for developmental retardation. The HOME was administered at ages six and 18 months. A discriminant function analysis was moderately sensitive in identifying low IQs; however, across time the HOME scores were less stable than previously reported.

2. Adams, M.M., Berg, C.J., Rhodes, P.H., & McCarthy, B.J. (1991). Another look at the black-white gap in gestation-specific perinatal mortality. *International Journal of Epidemiology, 20,* 950–957.
    Reasons for black infants' higher perinatal mortality rates were examined. Black infants had relatively better survival at 35–36 weeks of gestation. This advantage was reversed among infants of 39–41 and 42–43 weeks' gestation. For black infants with 39–41 weeks' gestation, the optimum BW was 187g greater than the median BW. For comparable white infants, the optimum BW was 397g greater than the median BW.

3. Adams, M.M., Rhodes, P.H., & McCarthy, B.J. (1990). Are race and length of gestation related to age at death in the sudden infant death syndrome? *Paediatric and Perinatal Epidemiology, 4,* 325–339.
    The relationships between race, preterm delivery, and SIDS were examined. The death rate for SIDS among black infants was twice that of white infants. How-

ever, the risk for all infants was smaller with gestations of less than 35 weeks. For black postneonates, the results do not support an association between length of gestation and age at death.

4. Aldous, M.B., & Edmonson, M.B. (1993). Maternal age at first childbirth and risk of low birth weight and pre-term delivery in Washington State. *Journal of the American Medical Association, 270,* 2574–2577.

The consequences of first childbearing after age 35 for white and black infants indicated that the chance for delivering an LBW white infant increased progressively with maternal age. There was no significant maternal age effect found among births of black infants; however, the sample was small. It is unclear if increasing maternal age at first childbirth is a risk factor for LBW and preterm delivery of black infants in the United States.

5. Allen, M.C., & Alexander, G.R. (1990). Gross motor milestones in pre-term infants: correction for degree of prematurity. *Journal of Pediatrics, 116,* 955–959.

The effect of premature delivery on gross motor milestone attainment was studied in 100 high-risk black and white preterm infants with normal motor outcomes. On average, black infants attained milestones before white infants. The attainment of motor milestones for the preterm infants approximated that of a control group of term infants. The results suggest that chronological age should be used to determine motor delay in very preterm infants.

6. Alo, C.J., Howe, H.L., & Nelson, M.R. (1993). Birth-weight-specific infant mortality risks and leading causes of death: Illinois, 1980–1989. *American Journal of Diseases of Children, 147,* 1085–1089.

A study of mortality rates (from 1980 through 1989 in Illinois) for white and black infants indicated that the higher morality rates for black infants were attributable to LBW and premature birth. The results suggest that efforts to reduce black mortality must go beyond reducing LBW and premature birth.

7. Als, H. (1977). The newborn communicates. *Journal of Communication, 27,* `66–73.

Observations of black mother-infant dyads were conducted on the 2nd and 3rd days after delivery. Mothers looked at their newborns about 80% of the time, smiled at their babies 34% of the time, and talked to the babies about 28% of the time. The infant's eyes were open about 50% of the time, with about 25% of that time in eye contact with mothers. Maternal behavior was dependent on the baby's state. A variety of infant behaviors were able to elicit responses from the mother.

8. Anderson-Yockel, J. (1994). Joint book-reading strategies in working-class African American and white mother-toddler dyads. *Journal of Speech & Hearing Research, 37,* 583–593.

African American and white mother-infant dyads were video-recorded while participating in three book-reading activities. The videotapes were analyzed to determine cultural differences and the effects of book familiarity on the occurrence of maternal and child communication behaviors. The results suggest many similarities between the groups; however, African American mothers used significantly fewer questioning behaviors, white children produced more question-related communications, and African American children produced more spontaneous verbalizations.

9. Atrash, H.K., Rowley, D., & Hogue, C.J. (1992). Maternal and perinatal mortality. *Current Opinion in Obstetrics and Gynecology, 4,* 61–71.

Mortality among black infants continues to be a problem. Interventions are needed to reduce preventable deaths of normal BW, LBW, and premature births among black infants. Research is needed to identify suitable interventions (i.e., better prenatal care, alternatives in deliveries). Maternal death also needs to be studied to understand causes and risk factors.

10. Aylward, G.P. (1981). The development course of behavioral states in pre-term infants: A descriptive study. *Child Development, 52,* 564–568.

Preterm black infants' longitudinal changes in observable states during a standardized neurologic examination were examined. Only observable behaviors were considered. The results suggest that the level of arousal increased as the examination progressed. Conceptional age seemed to dictate the rapidity of change from lower to higher states, and the predominant highest states were dependent on age.

11. Barclay, A. (1985). A factor analytic study of responses to the Bayley Scales of Infant Development by a disadvantaged population. *Perceptual & Motor Skills, 60,* 713–714.

The BSID was administered to 53 12- to 21-month-olds and 53 21- to 30-month-olds (*n* = 101 black infants). Factor analysis yielded six to four factors. Comprehension of verbal and gestural communication accounted for most of the variance for the younger group. Gross psychomotor behaviors accounted for variance in both age groups. The results were consistent with the notion of increasing differentiation of mental abilities with age.

12. Berg, C.J., Zupan, J., d'Almada, P.J., Khoury, M.J., & Fuller, L.J. (1994). Gestational age and intrauterine growth retardation among white and black very low birthweight infants: A population-based cohort study. *Paediatric and Perinatal Epidemiology, 8,* 53–61.

Characteristics of black and white VLBW infants were examined to identify differences in gestational ages and rates of fetal growth. The majority of the VLBW infants were born between 23 and 30 weeks, and all infants of 33 weeks' gestation or greater were growth retarded. There were no significant differences found between black and white infants. However, VLBW rate among black infants is more than three times greater than white infants.

13. Berlin, L.J., Brooks-Gunn, J., Spiker, D., & Zaslow, M.J. (1995). Examining observational measures of emotional support and cognitive stimulation in black and white mothers of preschoolers. *Journal of Family Issues, 16,* 664–686.

The Infant Health and Development Program was used to examine parenting behavior (PB) in mothers of 486 premature LBW infants (204 white and 282 black). PB was measured by the HOME. The PB predictive strengths were examined using two child outcomes: children's behavior problems and children's receptive language abilities up through age 36 months. The results suggest that there may be racial differences in the relation between PB and childhood functioning for white and black children.

14. Bertoli, F., Rent, C., & Rent, G. (1984). Infant mortality by socio-economic status for Blacks, Indians, and Whites: A longitudinal analysis of North Carolina, 1968–1977. *Sociology and Social Research, 68,* 364–377.

From 1968 to 1977, infant mortality rates among blacks, Native Americans, and whites in North Carolina were documented. All groups experienced reduced rates, but initial differentials persisted. Native Americans' infant mortality rate decreased most dramatically. Blacks and Native Americans experienced mortality in the neonatal period more often than whites. The Native American neonatal rate was more similar to whites than blacks, but their rate of postneonatal mortality was greater than that of blacks. Education was found to be the strongest predictor of infant mortality, particularly for whites.

15. Benasich, A.A., & Brooks-Gunn, J. (1996). Maternal attitudes and knowledge of child-rearing: Associations with family and child outcomes. *Child Development, 67(3)*, 1186–1205.

This study examined cognitive and behavioral outcomes in a cohort of LBW, preterm infants. Results suggest that home environment, maternal knowledge, and behavior problems were associated. However, child characteristics were not associated with maternal knowledge.

16. Billman, D.O., Nemeth, P.B., Heimler, R., & Sasidharan, P. (1996). Prenatal cocaine/polydrug exposure: Effect of race on outcome. *Journal of Perinatology, 16(5)*, 366–369.

The effect of prenatal exposure to cocaine on development is examined in black infants. It is concluded that when cocaine-exposed infants are compared to a control group that genetic differences may account for differences found between them.

17. Birns, B., & Golden, M. (1972). Prediction of intellectual performance at 3 years from infant tests and personality measures. *Merrill Palmer Quarterly, 18*, 53–58.

The social class and cognitive development of black infants were studied. The CIIS, the Piaget Object Scale, and seven personality rating scales were administered at 18 and 24 months and the Stanford-Binet at 36 months. The CIIS and Piaget scales were predictive of the infants' later intellectual performance on the Stanford-Binet. These findings indicate that discontinuity may exist between perceptual-motor development and later problem-solving ability on the verbal level, and that continuity may exist for certain personality traits related to both preverbal and verbal intelligence.

18. Black, M.M., Hutcheson, J.J., Dubowitz, H., Starr, R.H., Jr., & Berenson-Howard, J. (1996). The roots of competence: Mother-child interaction among low income, urban, African American families. *Journal of Applied Developmental Psychology, 17(3)*, 367–391.

The developmental competence and mother-child interaction during feeding and play were examined. Convergent validity was ascertained by comparing two parental factors; nurturance and control, and two child factors; interactive communication and affective regulation. An ecological theory relating parental nurturance and control to children's competence was used to test the construct validity of the observational procedure.

19. Blake, I.K. (1993). The social-emotional orientation of mother-child communication in African American families. Special Issue: International roots of minority child development. *International Journal of Behavioral Development, 16*, 443–463.

The longitudinal language development of black children was studied by observing children with their mothers in a low-structured communicative setting. Children's language developed in length and semantic-syntactic relations, which is similar to white children. Differences were found in the group patterns of semantic-syntactic relations, which suggests a social-emotional orientation style of communication. This pattern was the same for infant and mother, which suggests a cultural basis for this style.

20. Boone, M. (1982). A socio-medical study of infant mortality among disadvantaged Blacks. *Human Organization, 41*, 227–236.

Infant death and LBW delivery were studied in disadvantaged black women. Results show that within an inner-city black population, where educational levels are relatively low and much of the reproductive segment is young and unmarried, the standard at-risk identification criteria of age, education, and marital status do not vary with poor pregnancy outcome. Alcoholism, smoking, low maternal weight at delivery, hypertension history, migrant status, ineffective contraception, poor prenatal care, violence, and relatively poor psychological adjustments and social support systems were found to be salient predisposing factors.

21. Boone, M.S. (1985). Social and cultural factors in the etiology of low birth-weight among disadvantaged blacks. *Social Science and Medicine, 20,* 1001–1011.

Intensive exploratory interviews were conducted with black women whose infants had died by age one. In addition, 302 black obstetric inpatients and sub samples of women who had LBW and VLBW deliveries were studied. Prenatal care, alcoholism, migrant status, smoking, hypertension, and previous poor pregnancy outcome distinguished women with VLBW infants. The women also suffered from high levels of violence, weak social support systems, poor social and psychological adjustments, and ineffective contraception.

22. Bowering, J., Lowenberg, R.L., Morrison, M.A., Parker, S.L., & Tirado, N. (1978). Infant feeding practices in East Harlem. *Journal of the American Dietary Association, 72,* 148–155.

Infant feeding practices among low-income infants in East Harlem were surveyed prior to participation in a nutrition education program. Results show similar nutrient intakes for black and Puerto Rican infants, although some ethnic differences were observed in the types of milk and solid foods consumed. Black infants received formula for a longer period, whereas Puerto Rican infants were transferred to whole cow's milk at a younger age.

23. Bradley, R.H., & Caldwell, B.M. (1981). Home environment and infant social behavior. *Infant Mental Health Journal, 2,* 18–22.

The HOME was administered to black and white infants and their families to examine the validity of the HOME as a predictor of social behavior. The BSID was used to assess early social behavior. The findings suggest that a relationship exists between HOME scores and social behavior; however, the association seems to be stronger for females.

24. Bradley, R.H. (1984). A comparative study of the home environments of infants from single-parent and two-parent black families. *Acta Paedologica, 1,* 33–46.

The home environment of black families (29 single-parent and 29 two-parent) was assessed by the HOME when the infants were 6 to 24 months old. Two-parent families achieved significantly higher HOME scores than single-parent families on the Opportunities for Variety in Daily Stimulation and Emotional and Verbal Responsivity of Mother subscales. Further analyses indicated that HOME scores were differentially related to children's three-year IQ scores depending on presence or absence of a father. Mothers' education showed a higher association with infant IQ in single-parent families.

25. Bradley, R.H., Mundfrom, D.J., Whiteside, L., & Casey, P.H. (1994). A factor analytic study of the Infant-Toddler and Early Childhood versions of the HOME Inventory administered to white, black, and Hispanic American parents of children born pre-term. *Child Development, 65,* 880–888.

Factor analyses were conducted on the Infant-Toddler (IT) and Early Childhood (EC) versions of the HOME Inventory for 477 black, 299 white, and 94 Hispanic premature LBW children. On the IT-HOME, factor structures for blacks and whites were similar, while the structure for Hispanics involved a seven-factor solution. For the EC-HOME, six factors were retained for both blacks and whites.

26. Bradley, R.H., Whiteside, L., Mundfrom, D.J., & Bleuins-Knade, B. (1995). Home environment and adaptive social behavior among premature, low birth weight children: Alternative models of environmental action. *Journal of Pediatric Psychology, 20,* 347–362.

The relation between Caucasian, African American, and Hispanic children's home environments and their adaptive social behavior was examined. Results showed low to moderate associations between scores on the HOME at one and three years and adaptive social behavior at 30 and 36 months. Only sociocultural group status at 36 months contributed to the prediction of persistence and enthusiasm as observed in the laboratory setting.

27. Brenner, S.L., Fischer, H., & Mann-Gray, S. (1989). Race and the shaken baby syndrome: Experience at one hospital. *Journal of the National Medical Association, 81,* 183–184.

The relationship between shaken baby syndrome (SBS) and race was examined by reviewing 544 hospital child abuse reports for infants 18 months or younger. There were 20 infants in the SBS group, ranging in age from 15 days to 18 months. Eight of 87 white abused children had SBS; 12 of 447 black abused children had SBS. The disproportionate number of white to black SBS infants may be accounted for by racial differences in methods of punishing children.

28. Brinker, R., Baxter, A., & Butler, L. (1994). An ordinal pattern analysis of four hypotheses describing the interactions between drug-addicted, chronically disadvantaged, and middle-class mother-infant dyads. Special Issue: Children and poverty. *Child Development, 65,* 361–372.

African American mothers and their infants with developmental disabilities or at high risk for developmental disability were examined. Dyadic interactions were videotaped and rated for infant involvement and maternal responsivity. Four mothers showed less responsivity to infants over time as a function of drug addiction, poverty, or serious developmental delay. The findings also showed that mothers naturally increase their responsivity over time and the mothers' interactive sensitivity fluctuates in relation to infants' involvement in the interaction over time.

29. Broussard, E.R. (1995). Infant attachment in a sample of adolescent mothers. *Child Psychiatry & Human Development, 25,* 211–219.

The attachment of 38 (10 black) newborn infants of adolescent mothers was assessed using a modified Ainsworth Strange Situation. None of the black infants or infants aged 14+ months demonstrated secure attachment. In this sample, only about 23 infants were classified as securely attached, whereas about 65% of most infant samples are classified as securely attached.

30. Burchinal, M.R., Follmer, A., & Bryant, D. (1996). The relations of maternal social support and family structure with maternal responsiveness and child outcomes among African American families. *Developmental Psychology, 32(6),* 1073–1083.

Social support networks are related to proximal and distal measures of parenting style. Women with larger support networks were found to be more responsive and provide more stimulating home environments.

31. Burchinal, M.R., Roberts, J.E., Nabors, L.A., & Bryant, D.M. (1996). Quality of center child care and infant cognitive and language development. *Child Development, 67(2),* 606–620.

The relationship between quality of center-based child care and infant cognitive and language development were examined. Results suggest that quality of infant care is positively correlated with cognitive development, language development, and communication skills. Neither child nor family factors was found to moderate the association between child care quality and infant development.

32. Butler, O.R. (1992). The reduction of black infant mortality: An 18-month evaluation of three Tennessee Black Health Care Task Forces' demonstration projects. *Journal of Health and Social Policy, 3,* 59–80.

Pilot projects were conducted in counties where black infant mortality rates are extremely high. The goals of the projects were to target the needs of women and children who are indigent and receiving Medicaid by: (1) improving BW and survival rates of black infants, (2) reducing maternal morbidity, (3) enhancing participation in appropriate and timely prenatal intrapartum and postpartum services, (4) reducing the incidence of unplanned pregnancies among adolescents, and (5) increasing the utilization of family planning services.

33. Camp, B.W. (1984). Child-rearing attitudes and personality characteristics in adolescent mothers: Attitudes toward the infant. *Journal of Pediatric Psychology, 9,* 57–63.

Hispanic, black, and white adolescent mothers were interviewed about their attitudes toward their infants. Ethnic differences were present only on measures of cognitive functioning and one measure of authoritarian ideology. Most of the mothers expressed positive attitudes toward the pregnancy and toward the infant.

34. Capute, A.J., Shapiro, B.K., Palmer, F.B., Ross, A., & Wachtel, R.C. (1985). Normal gross motor development: The influences of race, sex and socio-economic status. *Developmental Medicine & Child Neurology, 27,* 635–643.

Black and white full-term infants were prospectively studied to assess attainment of 12 gross motor milestones (e.g., roll prone to supine, roll supine to prone, sit, stand, cruise, walk, walk backward, and run) in the first two years of life. There were no significant sex differences in age of attainment; however, black infants attained motor milestones earlier than white infants.

35. Carlson, D.B., LaBarba, R.C., Sclafani, J.D., & Bowers, C.A. (1986). Cognitive and motor development in infants of adolescent mothers: A longitudinal analysis. *International Journal of Behavioral Development, 9,* 1–13.

The cognitive and motor development of infants born to 58 teen mothers and a matched control group of 59 adult mothers was longitudinally studied. Black subjects experienced less favorable outcomes in terms of BW, cesarean section, and labor and delivery complications. Infants born to adolescent mothers scored significantly lower on the MDI of the BSID relative to controls. Home environments of infants born to adolescents were found to be significantly less nurturant than those of controls, and the HOME ratings for black infants were significantly lower than those for white infants.

36. Cintas, H.M. (1988). Cross-cultural variation in infant motor development. *Physical & Occupational Therapy in Pediatrics, 8,* 1–20.

This study presents specific culturally related examples of motor developmental variation and discusses the possible relationship of infant care practices, environmental stresses, and selective factors on early motor behavior. Findings of comparative studies of Caucasian infants and infants of presumed African heritage reared in North America are presented, and the developmental delay seen in Native American and Asian infants is discussed.

37. Coles, C.D., Smith, I., Fernhoff, P.M., & Falek, A. (1985). Neonatal neurobehavioral characteristics as correlates of maternal alcohol use during gestation. *Alcoholism: Clinical & Experimental Research, 9,* 454–460.

The effects of black, low SES, unmarried mothers' use of alcohol during pregnancy on newborn behavior was studied. Neonates who were exposed to alcohol during gestation displayed significant alterations in reflexive behavior, less mature motor behavior, and an increased activity level in comparison to unexposed infants. Infants whose mothers stopped drinking in the second trimester were superior to those whose mothers continued to drink throughout pregnancy in observed state control, need for stimulation, motor tone, tremulousness, and asymmetries in reflexive behavior.

38. Coles, C.D., Smith, I.E., & Falek, A. (1987). Prenatal alcohol exposure and infant behavior: Immediate effects and implications for later development. *Advances in Alcohol & Substance Abuse, 6,* 87–104.

The incidence and persistence of central nervous system-related behavioral alterations in three groups of infants born to low socioeconomic status black women was studied at three days of age. Infants exposed to alcohol were less optimal in neurobehavioral responses. Infants whose mothers continued to drink were significantly lower on orientation toward auditory and visual stimuli, motor performance, and autonomic regulation than nonexposed infants. Differences in orientation, motor performance, reflexive behavior, and autonomic control were predictive of mental and motor performance.

39. Coles, C.D., Platzman, K.A., Smith, I., & James, M.E. (1992). Effects of cocaine and alcohol use in pregnancy on neonatal growth and neurobehavioral status. *Neurotoxicology & Teratology, 14,* 23–33.

The effects of gestational cocaine and alcohol exposure on fetal growth and neonatal behavior of full-term infants born to primarily black, low-income women were studied. The BNBAS was used at 2, 14, and 28 days. BW and head circumference were negatively affected by cocaine. On the BNBAS, significant differences were noted for several abnormal reflexes and for autonomic stability for drug-exposed infants.

40. Coll, C.G., Spekoski, C., & Lester, B.M. (1981). Cultural and biomedical correlates of neonatal behavior. *Developmental Psychobiology, 14,* 147–154.

The BNBAS was administered to Puerto Rican, black, and white two-day-old, full-term healthy neonates. Puerto Rican infants scored lower on habituation, higher on orientation, and higher on maintaining their organization with increasing stimulation than black and white infants.

41. Collins, J.W. (1992). Disparate black and white neonatal mortality rates among infants of normal birth weight in Chicago: A population study. *Journal of Pediatrics, 120,* 954–960.

A study of normal BW of black and white infants was conducted to determine the effects of risk status and access to tertiary care on racial differences in neonatal mortality rates. Prematurity, growth retardation, congenital anomalies, low Apgar scores at five minutes, teenage mothers, and poverty were more common among black infants. The difference in mortality rate was greatest between black and white infants who showed none of these risk factors. Level of perinatal care available is an important determinant of neonatal chance of survival for normal BW urban black infants.

42. Collins, J.W., & David, R.J. (1992). Differences in neonatal mortality by race, income, and prenatal care. *Ethnicity and Disease, 2,* 18–26.

The degree to which the social and physical environment affects the association between prenatal care and black pregnancy outcome in Chicago was studied. Although adequate (compared to inadequate) prenatal care was associated with improved BW distribution independent of community income, only in moderate-income areas was it related to black neonatal survival. For term black infants who received adequate prenatal care, residence in impoverished areas was associated with a nearly fourfold greater neonatal mortality rate.

43. Contreras, J.M. (1995). Pregnant African American teenagers' expectations of their infants' temperament: Individual and social network influences. *Journal of Applied Developmental Psychology, 16,* 283–295.

Pregnant African American teenagers' expectations of their infants' temperament were examined. Difficult temperaments were expected by teenagers who were anxious and/or depressed. A more positive temperament was expected by teenagers who were more satisfied with current support resources and perceived their maternal relationships as more warm and accepting. Teenagers who had more accurate beliefs and knowledge about infant development and milestones had more positive expectations of their infants.

44. Davis, R.A. (1988). Adolescent pregnancy and infant mortality: Isolating the effects of race. *Adolescence, 23,* 899–908.

The role of high black teenage pregnancy rates in the disparity between black and white infant mortality rates was examined. Teenage pregnancy was associated with LBW births. This study suggests that poverty, not race, accounts for the difference in infant mortality. However, poverty was positively related to infant mortality only during the first month of life.

45. de Cubas, M.M., & Field, T. (1984). Teaching interactions of black and Cuban teenage mothers and their infants. *Early Child Development & Care, 16,* 41–56.

Cuban mothers demonstrated verbalization significantly more often than black mothers. The groups did not differ on maternal "hidden agendas." Adult mothers showed a more internal locus of control than teenage mothers. Infants of black teenage mothers vocalized significantly less often than infants of the other groups.

46. Dowling, P.T., & Fisher, M. (1987). Maternal factors and low birthweight infants: A comparison of blacks with Mexican Americans. *Journal of Family Practice, 25,* 153–158.

Compared the most potent predictor of infant mortality (LBW) among low-income black and Mexican American infants. The incidence of LBW was 16.6% for blacks and 5.9% for Mexican Americans, suggesting that the latter group enjoys some sociocultural protection from the effects of urban poverty in the United States.

47. Druschel, C.M., McCarthy, B.J., Lavoie, M.R., & Sikes, R.K. (1989). Trends in cause-specific infant mortality in Georgia. *Journal of the Medical Association of Georgia, 78,* 89–92.

Trends from 1960 to 1980–1982 were examined to determine where infant mortality reductions for normal BW infants were made in the past and where gaps remain. In the neonatal period, mortality was reduced by 66% for white and 76% for black infants. In the postneonatal period, overall reductions were smaller than in the neonatal period: 50% for white and 71% for black infants. The majority of the remaining gap resulted from excess mortality in the infection, injury, and SIDS categories. The widest gaps in infant mortality exist in the postneonatal period.

48. DuPlessis, H.M., Bell., R., & Richards, T. (1997). Adolescent pregnancy: Understanding the impact of age and race on outcomes. *Journal of Adolescent Health, 20(3),* 187–197.

The effects of maternal age and ethnicity on poor pregnancy outcomes were examined. The results suggest that African American women were more likely to have LBW and preterm infants. Overall, maternal age at delivery and ethnicity were associated with poor pregnancy outcomes.

49. Emanuel, I., Hale, C., & Berg, C. (1989). Poor birth outcomes of American black women: An alternative explanation. *Journal of Public Health Policy, 10,* 299–308.

An explanation for the higher proportion of LBW infants and infant mortality among black versus white cohorts is offered based on the mother's own development, not just current sociodemographic factors and prenatal care. In particular, the mother's intrauterine and childhood environment may interfere with her growth and development, affecting reproductive outcomes. In addition, adult urban environments impact pregnancies and fetal development.

50. Farran, D.C., & Ramey, C.T. (1977). Infant day care and attachment behaviors toward mothers and teachers. *Child Development, 48*, 1112–1116. (Also in *Annual Progress in Child Psychiatry & Child Development*, 310–318, 1978)

The responsiveness of children to two important attachment figures, mothers and day-care teachers, was examined. Twenty-three black infants raised in day care were observed with their mothers, teachers, and a stranger in the room in a situation designed to heighten attachment behavior. Results indicated that children overwhelmingly preferred to be near and to interact with their mothers rather than their teachers. This suggests that the attachment bond to the mother had indeed been formed. Moreover, the infants perceived their mothers as help givers when faced with a mildly difficult task.

51. Feldman, J.F., Brody, N., & Miller, S.A. (1980). Sex differences in non-elicited neonatal behaviors. *Merrill-Palmer Quarterly, 26*, 63–73.

This study examined sex differences in nonelicited newborn behaviors: states, activity levels, spontaneous behavior and specific motor patterns. Observations were conducted before and after feeding black infants, 48 to 96 hours after birth. Data indicate that neonatal behavior for which males exceed females is not predictive of subsequent sex-linked behaviors. The behaviors for which females exceeded males were oral and facial movements; males exceeded females in movements involving the large musculature. Differences suggested that circumcision may be responsible for some state disorganization in males.

52. Ferguson, R., & Myers, S.A. (1990). The effect of race on the relationship between fetal death and altered fetal growth. *American Journal of Obstetrics and Gynecology, 163*, 1222–1230.

This population study examined racial differences in the relationship between BW and fetal death. Black fetuses seem to be more sensitive than white fetuses to factors that adversely affect growth. It appears that continued use of "race-neutral" data for clinical management in racially heterogenous populations will not accurately predict the risk of stillbirth.

53. Fernandez, M. (1993). Ethnicity and effects of age gap between unmarried adolescent mothers and partners. *Journal of Adolescent Research, 8*, 439–466.

Ethnic differences in the effects of the age gap between unmarried adolescent mothers and their partners were examined. Partners of one out of five black adolescents were at least five years older than the unmarried adolescent; an age gap this large was reported by one out of four white mothers. Results suggested that the effects of large age gaps between unmarried adolescent mothers and their partners were potentially positive for children but negative for mothers among white but not necessarily black participants.

54. Field, T.M., Widmayer, S.M., Stringer, S., & Ignatoff, E. (1980). Teenage, lower-class, black mothers and their preterm infants: An intervention and developmental follow-up. *Child Development, 51*, 426–436.

Infants born to lower-class teenage black mothers were compared with full-term infants of teenage mothers and with term and preterm infants of adult mothers. Factors that placed the preterm infant of the teenage mother at greater risk at birth were small-for-date infant size and less realistic developmental milestones and child-rearing attitudes expressed by the mother.

55. Field, T.M. (1981). Videotaping effects on the behaviors of low income mothers and their infants during floor-play interactions. *Journal of Applied Developmental Psychology, 2*, 227–235.

Interaction behaviors and language measures of low-income black mothers and their infants were compared to floor-play situations in which the mother was aware and unaware of being videotaped. When the mothers were aware of being videotaped, they were more proximal to their infants, offered and demonstrated toys more frequently, engaged in more frequent interaction games, vocalized more frequently, emitted a greater number of words and declarative and imperative utterances, and their infants engaged in more constructive play.

56. Field, T. (1989). Sharing and synchrony of behavior states and heart rate in nondepressed versus depressed. *Infant Behavior & Development, 12, 357–376.*

The behavior states and heart rates of lower SES depressed and nondepressed black mothers and their three-month-old infants were assessed. Depressed mothers and their infants shared negative affective behavior states more often and positive behavior states less often than nondepressed dyads. The relation between maternal and infant heart rate was closer in nondepressed than depressed mothers.

57. Field, T. (1990). Teenage parenting in different cultures, family constellations, and caregiving environments: Effects on infant development. *Infant Mental Health Journal, 11, 158–174.*

Being a Cuban teenage mother, living in a nuclear family, and being a secondary caregiver were each associated independently with stronger social support systems and more positive child-rearing attitudes and mother-infant play interactions. Despite these early advantages, maternal stimulation and infant performance decreased over the second year of life irrespective of ethnic group, family constellation, and caregiving arrangements.

58. Field, T., Morrow, C., & Adlestein, D. (1993). Depressed mothers' perceptions of infant behavior. *Infant Behavior & Development, 16, 99–108.*

Lower SES black mothers with high and low depression scores were videotaped interacting with their infants. Infants of symptomatic mothers were coded more negatively. However, the symptomatic mothers coded their infants' behavior even more negatively than the observers did. In contrast, they coded their own behavior more positively than the observers did. Both groups of mothers underestimated their own negative behavior.

59. Field, T. (1995). Relative right frontal EEG activation in 3- to 6-month-old infants of "depressed" mothers. Special Section: Parental depression and distress: Implications for development in infancy, childhood, and adolescence. *Developmental Psychology, 31, 358–363.*

Brain electrical activity was recorded in a sample of depressed and nondepressed mothers and their three- to six-month-old infants. A greater number of depressed mothers and their infants versus nondepressed mothers and their infants displayed right frontal EEG asymmetry. Data indicate that the depressed affect exhibited by infants of depressed mothers is associated with a pattern of brain electrical activity similar to that found in inhibited infants and children and in chronically depressed adults.

60. Finkelstein, J.W., Finkelstein, J.A., Christie, M., Roden, M., & Shelton, C. (1982). Teenage pregnancy and parenthood: Outcomes for mother and child. *Journal of Adolescent Health Care, 3, 1–7.*

A comparison of black and white teenage mothers indicated that blacks had proportionally more pregnancies and later initial prenatal visits, and that the children of white teenagers had more acute illness visits during the two-year follow-up. When the age of the teenage mother was considered, the one-minute Apgar scores for the children of 14-year-olds were lower. The school drop-out rate was higher with increasing maternal age. The only finding in a comparison of the teen to the 20- to

30-year-old group was higher complication rates for pregnancy and delivery for the teen group.

61. Flaherty, M.J. (1988). Seven caring functions of black grandmothers in adolescent mothering. *Maternal Child Nursing Journal, 17,* 191–207.

Primary care activities of black grandmothers of young teen mothers were examined. Grandmothers' management of resources enabled the family to cope as it assumed the responsibility of a new baby. Coaching and assessment ensured adolescents' development in mothering roles and preparation for infant care. Nurturing and assigning were related to psychosocial development and encouraged development of secure mother-infant interactions when used appropriately.

62. Friedman, D.J., Cohen, B.B., Mahan, C.M., Lederman, R.I., Vezina, R.J., & Dunn, V.H. (1993). Maternal ethnicity and birthweight among blacks. *Ethnicity and Disease, 3,* 255–269.

The association between ethnicity and BW among black women in Massachusetts was examined. The study cohort consisted of black infants and a comparison group of non-Hispanic white infants. Black infants were categorized into six ethnic groups. Results indicate that black American infants have lower mean BW and generally higher levels of risk than other black ethnic groups. Compared to the white reference group, black Americans, other blacks, and West Indians have significantly elevated relative risks of LBW.

63. Gardner, G. (1984). Effects of social and family factors on viral respiratory infection and illness in the first year of life. *Journal of Epidemiology & Community Health, 38,* 42–48.

Infants were monitored through the first year of life for respiratory viral infection (VI) and illness. The relationship between VI and social and familial factors was examined. Results show no general patterns of association between VI and social or familial factors. Significantly higher rates of lower respiratory disease were observed in day care and low-SES infants. No convincing differences for VI or respiratory illness were seen when parental smoking was an isolated factor.

64. Gee, S.C., Lee, E.S., & Forthofer, R.N. (1976). Ethnic differentials in neonatal and postneonatal mortality: A birth cohort analysis by a binary variable multiple regression method. *Social Biology, 23,* 317–325.

This study examined ethnic differences in neonatal and postneonatal mortality in Spanish surname, white (non-Spanish), and nonwhite infants in the presence of all factors. Spanish surname and non-Spanish white infants had a neonatal mortality risk about 13% below average; nonwhite (primarily black) infants' rates were 30% above average. BW and legitimacy status were the most reliable indicators of infant mortality.

65. Gennaro, S., Tulman, L., & Fawcett, J. (1990). Temperament in pre-term and full-term infants at three and six months of age. *Merrill-Palmer Quarterly, 36,* 201–215.

Temperament differences in preterm infants and healthy full-term infants at three and six months were examined. High correlations among several sociodemographic and perinatal variables resulted in the use of race as a proxy variable. The preterm infant groups were generally rated more difficult than full-term infants at both three and six months. All infants were generally rated as less difficult at six months than at three months. Type of delivery and infant gender were not related to temperament ratings.

66. Geronimus, A.T. (1992). The weathering hypothesis and the health of African-American women and infants: Evidence and speculations. *Ethnicity and Disease, 2,* 207–221.

Difference in infant mortality rates were examined as a function of maternal age. The black-white infant difference in infant mortality rates is larger at older maternal ages than at younger ages. While African Americans and non-Hispanic whites differ on which maternal ages are associated with the lowest risk of neonatal mortality, within each population first births are most frequent at maternal ages with the lowest risk. The "weathering hypothesis" asserts that the health of African American women may begin to deteriorate in early adulthood as a physical consequence of cumulative socioeconomic disadvantage.

67. Givens, S.R., & Moore, M.L. (1995). Status report on maternal and child health indicators. *Journal of Perinatal and Neonatal Nursing, 9*, 8–18.
   This study examines why African American infants suffer a significantly higher risk of poor pregnancy outcome. Immunization rates for preschoolers remain low. Changing social conditions, including rising child poverty rates, high teenage birth rates, an increased rate of births to unmarried women, and higher levels of unintended pregnancy may be contributing to stalled progress.

68. Goldenberg, R.L., Cliver, S.P., Mulvihill., F.X., Hickey, C.A., Hoffman, H.J., Klerman, L.V., & Johnson, M.J. (1996). Medical, psychosocial, and behavioral risk factors do not explain the increased risk for low birth weight among black women. *American Journal of Obstetrics Gynecology, 175(5)*, 1317–1324.
   Various demographic, behavioral, housing, psychosocial, and medical characteristics were examined to determine what explains the difference in pregnancy outcome between low-income black and white women. White women had more of the risk factors for LBW than black women. However, the incidence of LBW was higher among black women.

69. Goldenberg, R.L., Cliver, S.P., Cutter, G.R., Hoffman, H.J., Cassady, G., Davis, R.O., & Nelson, K.G. (1991). Black-white differences in newborn anthropometric measurements. *Obstetrics and Gynecology, 78*, 782–788.
   The effect of ethnicity on BW was examined in black and white newborns. These data suggest that in this population, intrinsic and/or extrinsic factors associated with race account for most smaller black newborn measurements and for much of the racial difference in BW.

70. Goodman, S.H. (1992). Perinatal complications in births to low socioeconomic status schizophrenic and depressed women. *Journal of Abnormal Psychology, 101*, 225–229.
   Pregnancy and birth complications among predominately African American schizophrenic, depressed, and well women were studied. Maternal competence and the mother's diagnosis of schizophrenia significantly determined the likelihood of less adequate prenatal care and more complicated births. The results indicate the importance of an assessment not only of a disturbed woman's diagnosis, but also of her personal background and social competence in determining the likelihood of obstetrical complications.

71. Gottfried, A.W. (1976). Interrelationships among activity variables in one-year-old infants. *Perceptual & Motor Skills, 42*, 1103–1106.
   Forty-five black infants' activity levels were assessed during a structured free-play situation. Activity measures suggested multidimensional or specific components of activity. Results support the theoretical position that activity should be viewed not as homogeneous but as a differentiated construct.

72. Greenberg, D.N., Yoder, B.A., Clark, R.H., Butzin, C.A., & Null, D.M. (1993). Effect of maternal race on outcome of pre-term infants in the military. *Pediatrics, 91*, 572–577.

Outcomes for 392 white and 165 black infants were studied. Preeclampsia was more frequent in black mothers than in white mothers, but differences between races in BW remained after correction for preeclampsia. There were no significant differences between races in stillbirths, gender, maternal age, maternal transfer status, number of prenatal visits, or percentages of mothers with small-for-gestational-age infants, multiple-gestation infants, prolonged rupture of membranes, or initial prenatal visit during the first trimester.

73. Hale, C.B., & Druschel, C.M. (1989). Infant mortality among moderately low birth weight infants in Alabama, 1980 to 1983. *Pediatrics, 84,* 285–289.

Patterns of mortality among infants weighing 1500 g to 2499 g at birth and born in Alabama between 1980 and 1983 were examined for differences by race, residence, and cause of death. Neonatal, postneonatal, and infant mortality rates were higher for black infants. Neonatal mortality was highest for white infants from the rural part of the state; postneonatal mortality was highest for black infants from the rural part of the state.

74. Hanline, M.F. (1992). Family coping strategies and strengths in Hispanic, African-American, and Caucasian families of young children. *Topics in Early Childhood Special Education, 12,* 351–366.

This study examined the relationship between maternal perceptions of family coping strategies and family strengths in Hispanic, African American, and Caucasian families of young children with and without disabilities. The use of internal family coping strategies tended to be more predictive of family strengths than was the use of social supports outside the family for all three ethnic groups.

75. Hall, W.S. (1975). Story recall in young black and white children: Effects of racial group membership, race of experimenter, and dialect. *Developmental Psychology, 11,* 628–634.

This study tested the effects of racial group membership on unstructured and probed recall. Results show that whites performed better than blacks in standard English, blacks performed better than whites in black English vernacular, blacks tested in Black English vernacular were equivalent to whites tested in Standard English, and whites performed better in Standard English than in Black English vernacular. When probed with questions, there was an overall increase in the proportion of correct information for both racial groups.

76. Hans, S.L. (1989). Developmental consequences of prenatal exposure to methadone. Conference of the Behavioral Teratology Society, the National Institute on Drug Abuse, and the New York Academy of Sciences: Prenatal abuse of licit and illicit drugs (1988, Bethesda, Maryland). *Annals of the New York Academy of Sciences, 562,* 195–207.

This conference presented data on the neurobehavioral development of a cohort of low-income black two-year-olds who were prenatally exposed to methadone. Thirty-six opioid users in a low-dose methadone maintenance program and their 42 infants were compared with 43 mothers who used no opioids and their infants. The infants were assessed with the BNBAS at one day and four weeks and with the BSID at two years. Results indicate that methadone may have a small, direct teratological effect on growth and development. Instead of causing a behavioral deficit, methadone may make children more susceptible to impoverished environments.

77. Hans, S.L. (1990). Planning programmes for high-risk infants: A facet analysis of parent-infant communication. Special Issue: Facet theory. *Applied Psychology: An International Review, 39,* 457–478.

The Parent-Infant Observation Guide (PIOG) was used to screen for problems in parent-infant interaction among high-risk black mothers and their one-year-old infants. Sixty-five dyads were assessed again when the infant was age two. Mothers who were contingently responsive to their infants had infants who were cooperatively responsive to their mothers. Data support the mutuality of positive affect between parent and child. Initiation of communication had the most complex meaning for all PIOG maternal variables.

78. Harris, L.H., Roland, E.J., & McBarnett, Y. (1990). The state of infant health and its relationship to maternal prenatal health in the United States. *Journal of National Black Nurses' Association, 4,* 75–81.

The impact that maternal prenatal health, teenage pregnancy, and strategies to reduce infant mortality have on the general health of infants was examined. A comparison was made between the strategies used by the United States and those used by other industrialized nations who have been more successful in reducing their infant mortality rate.

79. Harsham, J., Keller, J.H., & Disbrow, D. (1994). Growth patterns of infants exposed to cocaine and other drugs in utero. *Journal of the American Dietetic Association, 94,* 999–1007.

Postnatal growth patterns of predominately black infants exposed to cocaine and other drugs in utero was examined. The mean BW of the study infants was significantly lower than that of comparison groups. Despite adequate nourishment, stunting in length continued through the first year, resulting in infants who were overweight for length.

80. Hobbs, D., & Wimbish, J. (1977). Transition to parenthood by black couples. *Journal of Marriage and the Family, 39,* 677–689.

The transition to parenthood for 38 black couples was examined using interview techniques. Mothers reported significantly more difficulty than fathers in adjusting to their infants. Of 15 potential predictor variables, fathers' adjustment was associated with: (1) postbirth marital satisfaction, (2) age of self, (3) whether pregnancy was planned/desired, (4) number of additional children desired, and 5) preference for sex of baby. Mothers' adjustment was associated with: (1) age of self and (2) age of baby.

81. Honig, A.S. (1991). Piagetian and psychometric development of 12-month-old disadvantaged infants in an enrichment program. Special Issue: Varieties of early child care research. *Early Child Development & Care, 68,* 71–87.

Disadvantaged black infants were compared to 16 infants who did not receive an intervention program. All were assessed on the CIIS and Piagetian Infancy Scales. No differences emerged for the CIIS, but program infants were differentiated from controls on the Piagetian Object Permanence and Means-Ends Scales.

82. Hossain, Z. (1993). Division of household labor and child care in dual-earner African-American families with infants. *Sex Roles, 29,* 571–583.

Involvement in infant care and in household work and the degree of support received for child care was examined in 63 middle- to lower-middle-income dual-earner African American couples. Analyses revealed traditionally gender-differentiated patterns of involvement in care giving and household work. Father involvement in child care and household activities did not vary as a function of whether mothers worked full-time or part-time.

83. Hossain, Z., & Roopnarine, J. (1994). African-American fathers' involvement with infants: Relationship to their functioning style, support, education, and income. *Infant Behavior & Development, 17,* 175–184.

African American fathers were less likely to engage in and devote time to basic caregiving activities than were mothers. Paternal investment in child care did not differ as a function of whether their wives worked full- or part-time. Fathers were more likely to invest time in play with the infant than in feeding or cleaning. Fathers' ability to communicate effectively within the family and their commitment to the family were significantly associated with their degree of involvement in feeding and comforting infants.

84. Howes, C., Sakai, L., Shinn, M., Phillips, D., Galinsky, E., & Whitebook, M. (1995). Race, social class, and maternal working conditions as influences on children's development. *Journal of Applied Developmental Psychology, 16*, 107–124.

African American and European American infant/preschool children were observed and their mothers interviewed to examine associations between maternal working conditions and child behavior. Results suggest that child-care quality could be predicted in both racial groups, but the patterns of association differed. Social class directly predicted child-care quality in European Americans, but did so indirectly through word demands for African Americans.

85. Hulsey, T.C., Levkoff, A.H., & Alexander, G.R. (1991). Birth weights of infants of black and white mothers without pregnancy complications. *American Journal of Obstetrics and Gynecology, 164*, 1299–1302.

An analysis of normal spontaneous vaginal deliveries was performed to examine racial differences in mean BW of infants whose mothers were without antepartum or intrapartum medical complications of pregnancy. When statistically significant differences in demographic characteristics were controlled, black infants had an average BW 181g less than that of white infants.

86. Hulsey, T.C., Levkoff, A.H., Alexander, G.R., & Tompkins, M. (1991). Differences in black and white infant birth weights: The role of maternal demographic factors and medical complications of pregnancy. *Southern Medical Journal, 84*, 443–446.

These investigators studied the association of racial disparities in mean BW with population differences in maternal demographic characteristics and antepartum-intrapartum medical complications. The mean BW for black infants was 214 g less than that for white infants. Black and white mothers differed significantly in marital status, age, and years of education. Black and white mothers also differed significantly in the incidence of chronic hypertension, preeclampsia-eclampsia, anemia, amnionitis, fever on admission, and sexually transmitted diseases.

87. Hummer, R. (1993). Racial differentials in infant mortality in the U.S.: An examination of social and health determinants. *Social Forces, 72*, 529–554.

The association between race and infant mortality was examined. The racial gap in infant mortality was nearly identical for endogenous and exogenous causes of death, with the overall rate among African Americans about 2.2 times higher than that for non-Hispanic whites.

88. Hutcheson, J.J., & Black, M.M. (1996). Psychometric properties of the Parenting Stress Index in a sample of low-income African American mothers of infants and toddlers. *Early Education & Development, 7(4)*, 381–400.

The study examined the consistency of the psychometric properties of the Parenting Stress Index. The results suggest that the Parenting Stress Index is consistent across samples that vary in ethnicity and socioeconomic status.

89. Jackson, J. (1986). Characteristics of black infant attachment behaviors. Second Annual Conference of the Black Task Force: The black family: Mental health perspectives (1984, San Francisco, California). *American Journal of Social Psychiatry, 6*, 32–35.

Attachment behavior between black infants and their parents was examined. Patterns of attachment behaviors were presented for the infants, who were at low risk of developing psychopathologies. Distinctive features of black infants' attachment behaviors were identified and discussed in relation to the extended network context of infant life.

90. Jackson, J.F. (1993). Multiple caregiving among African Americans and infant attachment: The need for an emic approach. *Human Development, 36,* 87–102.

The study of attachment among African American infants may need to consider cultural differences. Infant attachment may be misunderstood if traditional white middle-class cultural standards are used. An exploratory study of 37 African American infants found that they had 2 to 5 primary adult caregivers and a large set of secondary caregivers.

91. Jacobson, J.L., Jacobson, S.W., & Sokol, R.J. (1996). Increased vulnerability to alcohol-related birth defects in the offspring of mothers over 30. *Alcohol Clinical and Experimental Research., 20(2),* 359–363.

The investigators interviewed a group of mothers regarding their use of alcohol during pregnancy to determine effects on infant development. Among infants of younger and older mothers, alcohol-related deficits were seen most strongly in the offspring of women over 30 years of age. The results suggest that physiological changes associated with aging and/or chronic drinking may play an important role in alcohol-related birth defects.

92. Jacobson, S.W., Jacobson, J.L., Sokol, R.J., Martier, S.S., & Chiodo, L.M. (1996). New evidence for neurobehavioral effects of in utero cocaine exposure. *Journal of Pediatrics, 129(4),* 581–590.

Large drug exposure early in pregnancy was related to faster responsiveness on an infant visual expectancy test but to poorer recognition memory and information processing, deficits consistent with prior human and animal findings. These persistent neurobehavioral effects of heavy prenatal cocaine exposure appear to be direct effects of exposure and independent of effects on gestational age.

93. Jacobson, S.W., Jacobson, J., O'Neill, J.M., & Padgett, R.J. (1992). Visual expectation and dimensions of infant information processing. *Child Development, 63,* 711–724.

Six-month-old African American infants' expectations of a visual stimulus were related to developmental measures. Reaction time was related to eye fixation in tests that measured visual recognition memory (VRM) and presented objects of different shapes to the infant. Reaction time and infants' stimulus expectation predicted VRM novelty preference.

94. Jacobson, S.W., Jacobson, J.L., Sokol, R.J., & Martier, S.S. (1993). Prenatal alcohol exposure and infant information processing ability. *Child Development, 64,* 1706–1721.

Inner-city black infants born to teenage women were assessed in relation to maternal alcohol use during pregnancy. Prenatal alcohol exposure was not related to visual recognition memory or cross-modal transfer of information; however, it was associated with longer fixation duration, a measure indicative of slower, less efficient information processing. It was also related to lower scores on elicited play and longer periods of toy exploration, possibly due to slower cognitive processing as well. The effects on processing speed and elicited play were dose-dependent.

95. Jacobson, J.L., Jacobson, S.W., Sokol, R.J., & Martier, S.S. (1993). Teratogenic effects of alcohol on infant development. *Alcoholism: Clinical & Experimental Research, 17,* 174–183.

Effects of moderate-to-heavy prenatal alcohol exposure on performance on the BSID for 382 black 13-month-old infants were studied. Data suggest specific deficits related to the emergence of the ability to imitate modeled behavior and the development of standing and walking. The incidence of poor performance on the BMI more than doubled in children whose mothers averaged at least 0.5 ounces absolute alcohol per day during pregnancy.

96. Jacobson, J.L., Jacobson, S.W., & Sokol, R.J. (1994). Effects of prenatal exposure to alcohol, smoking, and illicit drugs on postpartum somatic growth. *Alcoholism: Clinical & Experimental Research, 18,* 317–323.

Physical growth from birth through 6.5 and 13 months was studied in 412 black inner-city infants recruited on the basis of their mothers' use of alcohol and/or cocaine during pregnancy. Prenatal alcohol exposure was associated with a slower rate of growth through 6.5 months of age. This postnatal growth retardation was associated with maternal drinking in the latter part of gestation, and was not related to drinking at the time of conception or to postnatal exposure to alcohol from breast feeding. Smoking and cocaine use during pregnancy were associated with faster postnatal weight gain.

97. Jacobson, J.L., Jacobson, S.W., Sokol, R.J., Martier, S.S., Ager, J.W., & Shankaran, S. (1994). Effects of alcohol use, smoking, and illicit drug use on fetal growth in black infants. *Journal of Pediatrics, 124,* 757–764.

The effects of prenatal exposure to alcohol, smoking, and illicit drugs on birth size of black infants were assessed. However, when all four substances, gestational age, and six covariates were controlled statistically, BW related only to alcohol and smoking, length only to alcohol, and head circumference only to opiates. Although smoking affected BW at all levels of exposure, a larger deficit was seen in relation to heavy drinking than to heavy smoking. Alcohol and smoking did not affect birth size synergistically, and their effects were seen primarily in infants of women over age 30.

98. Johnston, F.E., & Beller, A. (1976). Anthropometric evaluation of the body composition of black, white, and Puerto Rican newborns. *American Journal of Clinical Nutrition, 29,* 61–65.

White, black, and Puerto Rican infants one to five days old were measured for BW, length, triceps and subscapular skinfolds, and upper arm circumference. Females had greater skinfold thicknesses than males, but significant differences were found only for the triceps. Whites and blacks did not differ in skinfold thickness, but the Puerto Rican infants had significantly smaller triceps skinfolds.

99. Johnson, D., & Brody, N. (1977). Visual habituation, sensorimotor development, and tempo of play in one-year-old infants. *Child Development, 48,* 315–319.

The pattern of relationships between rate of visual habituation, sensorimotor development, play tempo, and motor activity was examined in 168 one-year-old black infants. For girls, longer fixation time to the initial stimulus presentation and faster habituation on the original series were associated with advanced sensorimotor development. Results suggest that both the sex and state of the infant are important moderators of the relationship between measures of visual attention and other individual difference variables.

100. Jones, G., Stockwell, E., & Wicks, J. (1982). Socioeconomic differences in infant mortality by race in Columbus, Ohio, 1969–71. *Black Sociologist, 9,* 48–55.

The association between SES and all measures of infant mortality for the total population was assessed. When examined separately by race, it appeared that the overall inverse relationship was due almost entirely to the experience of the white population. For nonwhites, none of the correlations were significant. Results for the total and white population revealed the increasing importance of family status rather than economic status as a salient factor; they also showed that the relationship has become as pronounced for neonatal as for postneonatal mortality.

101. Kaplan-Estrin, M., Jacobson, S.W., & Jacobson, J.L. (1994). Alternative approaches to clustering and scoring the Bayley Infant Behavior Record. *Infant Behavior & Development, 17,* 149–157.

Low-income black infants (*n* = 183) were assessed on the HOME at 12 months and on the BMI and IBR at 13 months. Ninety infants were retested at 25 months. Factor analysis of the IBR yielded three factors similar to those found for middle-class infants. Clusters related to affect and arousal, but not attention, were associated with HOME scores, suggesting that attention may be more constitutionally than environmentally based. Analyses of suspect ratings demonstrated the validity of this approach and indicated high suspect ratings for this sample on hyporeactivity.

102. Kempe, A., Wise, P.H., Barkan, S.E., Sappenfield, W.M., Sachs, B., Gortmaker, S.L., Sobol, A.M., First, L.R., Pursley, D., Rinehart, H., et al. (1992). Clinical determinants of the racial disparity in very low birth weight. *New England Journal of Medicine, 327,* 969–973.

Medical records of infants in various geographic regions who weighed 500 g to 1499 g were reviewed. The higher proportion of black infants with VLBW was related to an elevated risk in their mothers of major conditions associated with VLBW, idiopathic preterm labor, hypertensive disorders, and hemorrhage. The higher proportion of black infants with VLBW is associated with a greater frequency among black women of all major maternal conditions precipitating delivery.

103. Kennedy, J.H., & Bakeman, R. (1984). The early mother-infant relationship and social competence with peers and adults at three years. *Journal of Psychology, 116,* 23–34.

The impact of the early mother-infant relationship on social competence was studied in 39 black infants. The mother's responsiveness at three months was related to the child's later social competence with adults, whereas the infant's responsiveness to mother at three months was not correlated with measures of later social competence with either adults or with peers. Attachment classification at one year was related to the success of bids for interaction, complexity of bids, and whether the child spent time near peers or near adults at three years, as well as to camp staff members' ratings of social competence with peers and with adults.

104. Kerr, G.R., Ying, J., & Spears, W. (1995). Ethnic differences in causes of infant mortality: Texas births, 1989 through 1991. *Texas Medicine, 91,* 50–56.

Reducing adverse pregnancy outcomes in African American women will reduce but not resolve the racial discrepancy in infant mortality rates. Infant mortality rates for 30 of the top 59 causes of death were at least 1.5 times higher in African American than in Anglo and Hispanic infants, whereas a comparable excess in Hispanic infants was noted only for anencephaly.

105. King, T. (1982). Teenage mothers and their infants: New findings on the home environment. *Journal of Adolescence, 5,* 333–346.

This study investigated personality and social dimensions that might mediate the effects of white, black, and Hispanic teenagers' parenting. Results indicate that older parents provided more appropriate play materials and received higher ratings on the quality of stimulation offered the child. Minorities performed less well on the HOME, and of SES variables, only father's education was significantly related to total HOME scores. Subjects who scored higher on the KCDS tended to provide a more organized environment for their infants.

106. King, W.L., & Seegmiller, B. (1973). Performance of 14- to 22-month-old black, firstborn male infants on two tests of cognitive development: The Bayley scales and the Infant Psychological Development Scale. *Developmental Psychology, 8,* 317–326.

Fifty-one black infants were tested at three ages. The mean BMI score was elevated at 14 months but fell to a level similar to the standardization sample at 18 months and remained stable to 22 months. The mean BPI was significantly greater than that of the standardization sample at all age levels. The mental scale showed good predictive validity, whereas the psychomotor scale showed almost none. The Infant Psychological Developmental Scale appears to measure specific abilities and to be most applicable below 18 months of age. The BMI showed the greatest number of intercorrelations with all other scales at all age levels.

107. Kleinman, J., & Kessel, S. (1987). Racial differences in low birth weight: Trends and risk factors. *New England Journal of Medicine, 317,* 749–753.

The effects of maternal characteristics on rates of VLBW and MLBW were investigated. Maternal factors had directionally similar but quantitatively different effects on both VLBW and MLBW among blacks and whites. Fifteen percent of the decline in the MLBW rate among whites could be attributed to favorable changes in maternal characteristics. Among blacks, adverse changes in maternal characteristics accounted for 35% of the increase in the VLBW rate.

108. Kleinman, J.C., Fingerhut, L.A., & Prager, K. (1991). Differences in infant mortality by race, nativity status, and other maternal characteristics. *American Journal of Diseases of Children, 145,* 194–199.

The objective of this study was to examine the effects of nativity status (native- vs. foreign-born) and other maternal characteristics (age, parity, education, and marital status) on infant, neonatal, and postneonatal mortality among whites and blacks. Neonatal mortality risk was 22% lower among the black foreign-born mothers than among the black native-born mothers, whereas among white infants, there was no risk difference by nativity. If the infant mortality rate in the low-risk groups could be achieved by the moderate- and high-risk groups, there would be a 30% reduction in infant deaths within each race.

109. Klonoff-Cohen, H.S., & Edelstein, S.L. (1995). A case-control study of routine and death scene sleep position and sudden infant death syndrome in southern California. *Journal of the American Medical Association, 273,* 790–794.

This study investigated whether infants who died of SIDS were routinely placed in different sleep positions compared with healthy infants in a multiethnic diverse population in the United States. There was no difference in routine sleep position for SIDS infants and comparison infants. Hispanic parents routinely placed their infants on their abdomens less frequently than white parents. However, the prone sleep position was the most commonly found sleep position at death in both Hispanic and non-Hispanic infants.

110. Kovar, M.G. (1977). Mortality of black infants in the United States. *Phylon, 38,* 370–397.

Data from the vital registration system of the United States demonstrate very clearly that infant mortality rates have declined more for late than for early infant deaths and that the rate of decline at early ages has been significantly less for black than for white infants. A great deal of variation in black infant mortality rates occurs among different geographic areas. The greatest number of deaths could be prevented in the rural South and in the counties constituting the cores of cities in the North Central and Northeast regions.

111. Kugler, J.P., Connell, F.A., & Henley, C.E. (1990). Lack of difference in neona-

tal mortality between blacks and whites served by the same medical care system. *Journal of Family Practice, 30,* 281–288.

This study examined the influence of health care systems on racial differences in LBW and neonatal mortality. Black infants had significantly higher rates of LBW than white infants. Black infants served by civilian medical care had approximately twice the neonatal mortality of white infants; however, black infants born in the military hospital had a neonatal mortality rate comparable to white infants. Controlling for marital status, age, parity, and income status did not appreciably change these patterns. The effect was most prominent for normal weight black infants, especially for those from low-income census tracts.

112. Landerholm, E. (1984). Teenage parenting skills. *Early Child Development & Care, 13,* 351–364.

The relationship between infant sex and teenage mother-infant interactions was investigated. Mothers of female infants called their child's name and demonstrated toy use significantly more often and used significantly more object/material play to get their child's attention than mothers of male infants. Mothers of male infants were significantly more affectionate and physical than mothers of female infants.

113. Lanehart, R., Clark, H., Kratochvil, D., Rollings, J., & Fidora, A. (1994). Case management of pregnant and parenting female crack and polydrug abusers. *Journal of Substance Abuse, 6,* 441–448.

The relationship between service components of a comprehensive treatment program and substance-free time among 120 African American and Caucasian crack-cocaine-addicted women was studied. Findings indicate that the relationship was significant for aftercare management vocational services and residential treatment. Findings support a growing body of literature suggesting that crack- and poly-drug-using women can be responsive to treatment.

114. Langkamp, D.L., Foye, H.R., & Roghmann, K.J. (1990). Does limited access to NICU services account for higher neonatal mortality rates among blacks? *American Journal of Perinatology, 7,* 227–231.

This study examined the admissions of black LBW newborns to the NICU. Higher black neonatal mortality rates did not appear to be due to limited access to NICU services, but more normal BW black babies may have died of potentially preventable causes.

115. Langlois, J., Ritter, J., & Casey, R. (1991). Maternal and infant demographics and health status: A comparison of black, Caucasian, and Hispanic families. *Journal of Biosocial Science, 23,* 91–105.

The relationships among ethnicity, demographics, smoking and drinking habits, and maternal and infant health were examined in low-income black, Caucasian, and Hispanic families. Few ethnic differences in the health of the mothers and their infants emerged when differences were directly examined; however, analyses indicated that Caucasian mothers were more likely to smoke and drink.

116. Leadbeater, B.J., Bishop, S.J., Raver, C.C. (1996). Quality of mother-toddler interactions, maternal depressive symptoms, and behavior problems in preschoolers of adolescent mothers. *Developmental Psychology, 32(2),* 280–288.

Maternal depressive symptoms, mother-toddler conflicts and maternal reports of child problem behavior were examined in a longitudinal study. An additive model best predicted child problem behavior. These findings suggest that maternal depressive symptoms and maternal-child conflict contribute independently to child problem behavior.

117. Leland, N.L., Petersen, D.J., Braddock, M., & Alexander, G.R. (1995). Variations in pregnancy outcomes by race among 10- to 14-year-old mothers in the United States. *Public Health Reports, 110,* 53–58.

This study examined variations in pregnancy outcomes among 38,551 black and white adolescents. The birthrate was 4.29 per 1,000 for blacks, more than seven times the rate for whites. Black mothers had higher proportions of VLBW and LBW infants than did whites. Neonatal and infant mortality rates were higher among VLBW and LBW white infants. Neonatal and infant mortality rates were similar for normal BW infants of both races. There were no differences by race for neonatal, postneonatal, and infant mortality. Young black adolescents appear to be particularly vulnerable to the already elevated risks for teenagers.

118. Lester, B.M. (1978). The organization of crying in the neonate. *Journal of Pediatric Psychology, 3,* 122–130.

The results of two studies are presented. One illustrates neonatal cry patterns that are possible correlates of fetal malnutrition, and the other compares the cries of high- and low-risk newborn infants (full BW, full term). It is concluded that the infant cry may be a useful indicator of risk but has not been shown to be of specific diagnostic utility.

119. Levin, J.S., Markides, K.S., Richardson, J.C., & Lubin, A.H. (1989). Exploring the persistent black risk of low birthweight: Findings from the GLOWBS study. *Journal of the National Medical Association, 81,* 253–260.

Black infants have significantly lower mean BW and higher risk of LBW than either Anglos or Hispanics. Despite controlling for a variety of pregnancy- and health-related, psychosocial, socioeconomic, and health services factors, being black still exerts a significant, inverse effect on BW.

120. Liaw, F., & Brooks-Gunn, J. (1993). Patterns of low-birth-weight children's cognitive development. *Developmental Psychology, 29,* 1024–1035.

The developmental patterns of cognitive performance was investigated over the first 3 years in a large sample of black and white LBW, premature children. Results reveal that these patterns of cognitive development can be discriminated by children's neonatal health status and treatment. Mother's cognitive ability and quality of a child's home environment were also found to be associated with LBW children's developmental patterns.

121. Lieberman, E., Ryan, K., Monson, R., & Schoenbaum, S. (1987). Risk factors accounting for racial differences in the rate of premature birth. *New England Journal of Medicine, 317,* 743–748.

Interview and medical record data were used to investigate medical and socioeconomic risk factors that may explain the increase in premature births among black women. Among the medical conditions examined, only the maternal hematocrit level (or some related factor) explained a substantial proportion of the increased rate of premature births to black women. When the number of the four socioeconomic risk factors were taken into account, essentially all of the racial variation in prematurity was explained.

122. Luke, B., Williams, C., Minogue, J., & Keith, L. (1993). The changing pattern of infant mortality in the U.S.: The role of prenatal factors and their obstetrical implications. *International Journal of Gynaecology and Obstetrics, 40,* 199–212.

Infant mortality rate has slowed due to a deterioration in the distribution of birth weights and a slowed improvement in BW-specific mortality rates. These effects are magnified when evaluated on a race-specific basis; the rate of LBW is twice as high and the rate of VLBW is three times as high for black infants compared to white infants. Reducing the rates of VLBW and LBW, particularly among blacks, holds the greatest potential for future reductions in infant mortality in the United States. The important role of maternal factors in the antecedents of infant mortality have been clearly and repeatedly demonstrated.

123. Lozoff, B., Askew, G.L., & Wolf, A.W. (1996). Co-sleeping and early childhood sleep problems: Effects of ethnicity and socioeconomic status. *Journal of Developmental & Behavioral Pediatrics, 17(1),* 9–15.

Results suggest that Caucasian mothers who coslept consider their child's sleep behavior to be problematic. These differences may be due to differing child rearing attitudes and expectations regarding child sleep behavior.

124. Malina, R. (1988). Racial/ethnic variation in the motor development and performance of American children. 18th Annual Meeting of the Canadian Association of Sport Sciences (Quebec, Canada). *Canadian Journal of Sport Sciences, 13,* 136–143.

There is evidence that black infants are advanced in motor development during the first 2 years of life, and that black school-age children, particularly boys, perform consistently better than white and Mexican American children in running speed (dashes) and the vertical jump. It is argued that a biocultural approach is required to systematically analyze data on motor performance, sociocultural factor, and various morphological, physiological, and biochemical parameters. (In French)

125. Mangold, W., & Powell-Griner, E. (1991). Race of parents and infant birthweight in the United States. *Social Biology, 38,* 13–27.

Social, demographic, ethnic, and genetic influences on race differences in BW were investigated. BW differences among infants with white, black, and mixed black-white parents indicate that those with two black parents had the lowest BW and those with two white parents had the highest. Parental educational attainment, prenatal care, and other social factors also affected BW differences.

126. Marcus, J., Hans, S.L., & Jeremy, R.J. (1983). Differential motor and state functioning in newborns of women on methadone. *Annual Progress in Child Psychiatry & Child Development,* 473–480.

This study assessed motor and state functioning of 20 infants born to methadone-maintained women and 25 born to controls at 1 day and 1 month of age using the BNBAS with Kansas Supplements. Results suggest a relationship between motor and state functioning, with motor functioning discriminating much more clearly between methadone and nonmethadone infants than state functioning. Both groups generally improved with age, but nonmethadone infants maintained some of their advantage in motor functioning.

127. Marcus, J., Hans, S.L., Patterson, C.B., & Morris, A.J. (1984). A longitudinal study of offspring born to methadone-maintained women: I. Design, methodology, and description of women's resources for functioning. *American Journal of Drug & Alcohol Abuse, 10,* 135–160.

Eighteen methadone-maintained (MM) black women and a comparison group of 24 nonmethadone black women were interviewed during their last trimester of pregnancy and at a four-month follow-up. The MM women were more likely to receive public assistance, display psychiatric dysfunctioning, and be less educated. They appeared committed to their methadone treatment and, in general, viewed their pregnancies in positive terms.

128. Markides, K., & Hazuda, H. (1980). Ethnicity and infant mortality in Texas counties. *Social Biology, 27,* 261–271.

An ecological analysis of infant mortality rates found associations between SES variables and infant mortality rates. A significant negative correlation emerged between neonatal mortality and percent Spanish surname was retained, even when the effects of other relevant variables (percent black, percent urban, & percent below poverty) were controlled.

129. Marsiglio, W., & Mott, F. (1988). Does wanting to become pregnant with a first child affect subsequent maternal behaviors and infant birth weight? *Journal of Marriage and the Family, 50,* 1023–1036.

The relationship between women's desire to become pregnant with their first child and their subsequent maternal behaviors and infant's BW was studied. Being black or younger was associated with below-average levels of pregnancy desire, whereas living in an urban area was positively associated with pregnancy desire. Women who desired pregnancy were more likely to initiate early prenatal care and to gain excessive weight during pregnancy. Desire was not a significant predictor of other behaviors and characteristics, including alcohol and smoking behavior.

130. May, J.W. (1983). Effects of age on color preference for black and white by infants and young children. *Perceptual & Motor Skills, 56,* 323–330.

The effect of race on color (black and white) preference by infants and young children was studied. A color preference test was administered to 160 children (aged 6 months to 4.5 years) who attended day care centers. Race and age appeared to interact in color preference; as age increased, black children showed a clear increase in their preference for the color white. A corresponding analysis for whites did not show a significant change in color preference with an increase in age.

131. Mayberry, R.M., & Lewis, R.F. (1990). Ten-year changes in birthweight distributions of black and white infants, South Carolina. *American Journal of Public Health, 80,* 724–726.

This study compared the BW distributions of black and white infants in South Carolina for the paired-year periods 1975–1976 and 1985–1986. No changes were found in BW between the two periods among black infants, but the white infants reflected an overall improvement.

132. Michielutte, R., Moore, M.L., Meis, P.J., Ernest, J.M., & Wells, H.B. (1994). Race differences in infant mortality from endogenous causes: A population-based study in North Carolina. *Journal of Clinical Epidemiology, 47,* 119–130.

The associations between race, BW, and mortality from endogenous causes were examined. Black infants were found to have approximately twice the mortality risk of white infants. The association between race and endogenous mortality differs within categories of medical etiology. The mortality risk is the same for black and white infants born preterm due to premature rupture of the membranes, lower for black infants born preterm due to medical problems, and higher for black infants born preterm due to idiopathic premature labor.

133. Miles, M.S., Burchinal, P., Holditch-Davis, D., Wasilewski, Y. (1997). Personal, family, and health-related correlates of depressive symptoms in mothers with HIV. *Journal of Family Psychology, 11(1),* 23–34.

This study examined the depressive symptoms mostly of African American mothers. The examination revealed that the best predictors of depressive symptoms were feelings of stigma, self-perceptions of health, and physical symptoms.

134. Mittendorf, R., Williams, M.A., Kennedy, J.L., Berry, R.E., Herschel, M., Aronson, M.P., & Davidson, K.M. (1993). A hypothesis to explain paradoxical racial differences in neonatal mortality. *American Journal of Preventive Medicine, 9,* 327–330.

Results indicate that black infants' gestations were about four days shorter than white infants'. However, after stratifying by BW, there was a reversal such that LBW black infants' gestations were seven days longer than the gestations of LBW white infants.

135. Murray, J.L. (1988). The differential effect of prenatal care on the incidence of low birth weight among blacks and whites in a prepaid health care plan. *New England Journal of Medicine, 319,* 1385–1391.

A review of data from black and white babies whose mothers' ages and levels of education were comparable indicated that black mothers used prenatal care less and had more infants with LBW than white mothers. The difference in the use of prenatal care accounted for less than 15% of the difference in the incidence of LBW. The rates of LBW, VLBW, and preterm birth decreased with increasing levels of prenatal care for both blacks and whites.

136. Mustin, H.D., Holt, V.L., & Connell, F.A. (1994). Adequacy of well-child care and immunizations in U.S. infants born in 1988. *Journal of the American Medical Association, 272,* 1111–1115.

The purpose of this study was to determine adequacy of preventive care and to identify risk factors for inadequate receipt of care using a national sample of U.S. infants. Adequate well-child visits were made by 82% of white infants and 75% of black infants; adequate immunizations were received by 46% and 34%, respectively. Sixty percent of infants who did not have adequate immunizations by 8 months had at least three well-baby visits. With adjustment for maternal education level, poor white children were 1.5 times more likely to receive inadequate care as infants in families with incomes greater than 185% of the federal poverty level.

137. Norbeck, J.S., DeJoseph, J.F., & Smith, R.T. (1996). A randomized trial of an empirically-derived social support intervention to prevent low birthweight among African American women. *Social Science and Medicine, 43(6),* 947–954.

This study examined the effect of an intervention designed to imitate the support usually provided by the pregnant woman's family. Results show that the incidence of LBW was less among intervention participants than controls.

138. Pedersen, F.A., Rubenstein, J.L., & Yarrow, L.J. (1979). Infant development in father-absent families. *Journal of Genetic Psychology, 135,* 51–61.

Fifty-five low-SES black infants were studied. Male infants who had experienced minimal interaction with their fathers were significantly lower on the BMI and on measures of social responsiveness, secondary circular reactions, and preferences for novel stimuli. Female infants appeared unaffected by the father's presence or absence.

139. Phillips, R.T. (1986). The effects of divorce on black children and adolescents. Second Annual Conference of the Black Task Force: The black family: Mental health perspectives (1984, San Francisco, California). *American Journal of Social Psychiatry, 6,* 69–73.

The literature on the developmental effects of divorce on black children was reviewed. It is suggested that the degree to which infants and toddlers are affected by divorce depends on how the mother is affected and how well she is able to resolve the crisis. As the child approaches age 5, divorce may have more of an impact on development. It is noted that there is little research data available on the effects of divorce on children and almost none on ethnic and racial differences.

140. Porter, R.H., Boyle, C., Hardister, T., & Balogh, R.D. (1989). Salience of neonates' facial features for recognition by family members. *Ethology & Sociobiology, 10,* 325–330.

The investigators examined the role of facial-visual cues in the recognition of black and white neonates by family members with neonate facial features masked or isolated. Results show that (1) photographs are accurately discriminated by close biological relatives; (2) a view of the entire face is not required by mothers to accurately discriminate photographs of their own versus infants of the same sex, age, and race; and (3) isolated photographs of eyes, nose, mouth, or head shape were recognized by mothers.

141. Powell-Griner, E. (1988). Differences in infant mortality among Texas Anglos, Hispanics, and blacks. *Social Science Quarterly, 69,* 452–467.

A large singleton birth cohort was used to examine the effects of BW, prenatal care, parental occupation, and marital status on risk of infant death among Texas Anglos, Hispanics, and Blacks. Hazards analysis indicates that each of these factors has a net effect on infant death. LBW is less of a disadvantage for black infants, prenatal care has the greatest impact on normal-weight infants' survival, and the selective effects of BW lessen with age.

142. Ramey, C.T., Farran, D.C., & Campbell, F.A. (1979). Predicting IQ from mother-infant interactions. *Child Development, 50,* 804–814.

Mothers of high-risk infants attending day care interacted with their infants in ways quite similar to mothers of high-risk infants not attending day care. Both high-risk groups differed from the general population of mothers on interaction and attitudinal measures. Children's intelligence at 36 months was predictable from previous maternal behaviors and attitudes, particularly for the control group, and early day care intervention apparently altered the predictiveness of some maternal factors.

143. Rao, R.P. (1993). Stress and coping among mothers of infants with a sickle cell condition. *Children's Health Care, 22,* 169–188.

Mothers of infants with sickle cell anemia and mothers of infants with sickle cell trait were interviewed in a study of the psychological stress and coping strategies they used. Mothers of children with sickle cell disease most often reported the expectation of pain for their child as a stressor, whereas mothers of children with sickle cell trait most often reported uncertainty of the diagnosis as a stressor.

144. Rawlings, J.S., & Weir, M.R. (1992). Race- and rank-specific infant mortality in a U.S. military population. *American Journal of Diseases of Children, 146,* 313–316.

Mortality among black infants in the United States is approximately twice that among white infants. The disparity has been attributed in large part to the higher incidence of poverty and limited access to health care among black Americans. The lower rates of mortality among black infants in this study may be due to guaranteed access to health care and higher levels of family education and income in the multiracial subpopulation served by our medical center compared with the nation as a whole.

145. Rawlings, J.S., Rawlings, V.B., & Read, J.A. (1995). Prevalence of low birth weight and pre-term delivery in relation to the interval between pregnancies among white and black women. *New England Journal of Medicine, 332,* 69–74.

A racially mixed population of women in military families, who had access to free, high-quality health care, was studied. Short interpregnancy intervals (calculated from delivery to the next conception) were more frequent among black than white women. A short interval between pregnancies is a risk factor for LBW and preterm delivery.

146. Reeb, K.G., Graham, A.V., Zyzanski, S.J., & Kitson, G.C. (1987). Predicting low birthweight and complicated labor in urban black women: A biopsychosocial perspective. *Social Science & Medicine, 25,* 1321–1327.

Demographic, biomedical, and psychosocial factors were investigated as potential predictors of intrapartum complications and LBW in pregnant urban black women. Low family functioning, stressful events, Quetelet's Index, and cigarette smoking predicted LBW. Family functioning alone predicted LBW with 65% sensitivity, 64% specificity, and 31% positive predictive value.

147. Robert, J.E., Burchinal, M.R., Medley, L.P., Zeisel, S.A., Mundy, M., Roush, J., Hooper, S., Bryant, D., & Henderson, F.W. (1995). Otitis media, hearing sensitivity, and maternal responsiveness in relation to language during infancy. *Journal of Pediatrics, 126,* 481–489.

The relation between hearing loss associated with otitis media with effusion (OME) and language and cognitive skills at age one was studied in black infants attending community-based child care programs. The direct association between OME-related hearing loss and all language and cognitive measures was negligible. Children with more frequent hearing loss tended to have less responsive mothers and home environments, and this association was linked to lower performance on the infant assessments.

148. Rosenblith, J.F. (1974). Relations between neonatal behaviors and those at eight months. *Developmental Psychology, 10,* 779–792.

To determine whether newborn behavioral assessments are related to assessments at 8 months, a replication sample design was used with four samples of a nearly randomly chosen clinic population of newborns. Relations were examined separately for males and females, blacks and whites, and within each of four gestational age categories. Many relations between scores on the Neonatal Examination and performance at eight months were significant.

149. Roth, J., Resnick, M.B., Ariet, M., Carter, R.L., Eitzman, D.V., Curran, J.S., Cupoli, J.M., Mahan, C.S., & Bucciarelli, R.L. (1995). Changes in survival patterns of very low-birth-weight infants from 1980 to 1993. *Archives of Pediatrics and Adolescent Medicine, 149,* 1311–1317.

Race, sex, and transport status correlated significantly with survival of VLBW infants. Survival percentages were higher among black infants, female infants, and infants transported to perinatal intensive care centers than among white infants, male infants, and those admitted initially to the tertiary care centers.

150. Rowley, D.L. (1994). Research issues in the study of very low birthweight and preterm delivery among African-American women. *Journal of the National Medical Association, 86,* 761–764.

This study describes a research strategy designed to reduce the high infant mortality rate experienced by African American women relative to white women. The strategy focuses on improving poor health outcomes, understanding the unique factors that contribute to excess mortality rates, and involving women and their communities in defining and shaping research agendas.

151. Rowley, D.L. (1995). Framing the debate: Can prenatal care help to reduce the black-white disparity in infant mortality? *Journal of the American Medical Women's Association, 50,* 187–193.

Normal BW black infants have higher rates of death due to infections, injuries, and SIDS. VLBW black infants account for the increasing racial differences in infant mortality. Social determinants of the disparity in infant mortality include poverty and the accompanying problems of limited access to health care services, preventive care, and good nutrition. Prenatal care may reduce the disparity by using both high-risk and population-based prevention strategies.

152. Sagatun-Edwards, I., Saylor, C., & Shifflett, B. (1995). Drug exposed infants in the social welfare system and juvenile court. *Child Abuse and Neglect, 19,* 83–91.

This study examines how drug-exposed infants were processed, following a positive toxicology screen, through the social services and juvenile court system. Results indicate that African American and Hispanic cases were overrepresented and Caucasian and Asian cases were underrepresented. A petition to juvenile court was filed in almost 50% of the initial cases. Among children who were made dependents of the court, about 80% were removed from the mother and placed in reunification services. Of these, 33% were later returned to the family, and the rest went to permanent placements outside the home.

153. Sameroff, A., Bakow, H., McComb, N., & Collins, A. (1978). Racial and social class differences in newborn heart rate. *Infant Behavior and Development, 1,* 199–204.

Black babies were found to have much higher heart rates than white babies. When SES was considered, no heart rate difference was found between black and white infants in the poorest social class. In addition, neither the emotional nor the physical health of the mothers or infants was related to newborn heart levels.

154. Saylor, C.F., Casto, G., & Huntington, L. (1996). Predictors of developmental outcomes for medically fragile early intervention participants. *Journal of Pediatric Psychology, 21(6),* 869–887.

Developmental outcomes for medically fragile infants were examined in a longitudinal study. Results suggest that it is twice as expensive to begin sensorimotor intervention at an earlier age and assessments revealed no significant difference in developmental outcomes based on an earlier intervention start.

155. Schoendorf, K.C., Hogue, C.J., Kleinman, J.C., & Rowley, D. (1992). Mortality among infants of black as compared with white college-educated parents. *New England Journal of Medicine, 326,* 1522–1526.

In contrast to black infants in the general population, black infants born to college-educated parents have higher mortality rates than similar white infants only because of their higher rates of LBW. Black and white infants of normal BW have equivalent mortality rates.

156. Schoendorf, K.C., & Kiely, J.L. (1992). Relationship of sudden infant death syndrome to maternal smoking during and after pregnancy. *Pediatrics, 90,* 905–908.

Infants who died of SIDS were more likely to be exposed to maternal cigarette smoke than were surviving infants. Among black infants, the odds ratio was 2.4 for passive exposure and 2.9 for combined exposure; among white infants, the odds ratio was 2.2 for passive exposure and 4.1 for combined exposure. These data suggest that both intrauterine and passive tobacco exposure are associated with an increased risk of SIDS.

157. Seagull, F.N., Mowery, J.L., Simpson, P.M., Robinson, T.R. (1996). Maternal assessment of infant development: Associations with alcohol and drug use in pregnancy. *Clinical Pediatrics, 35(12),* 621–628.

This study examined whether maternal perceptions of infant development was associated with intake of alcohol or drugs. The results suggest that mothers who use alcohol and drugs are more likely to overestimate their infants' mental and physical development.

158. Seegmiller, B.R., & King, W.L. (1975). Relations between behavioral characteristics of infants, their mothers' behaviors, and performance on the Bayley Mental and Motor Scales. *Journal of Psychology, 90,* 99–111.

BMI scores were significantly related to several concurrent ratings of infant and maternal behavior in a sample of firstborn black male infants aged 14, 18, or 22 months. By 22 months, infants scoring higher on the BMI had mothers who were more highly involved with their child's achievement.

159. Segal, L.B., Oster, H., Cohen, M., Caspi, B., Myers, M., & Brown, D. (1995). Smiling and fussing in seven-month-old preterm and full-term black infants in the still-face situation. *Child Development, 66,* 1829–1843.

Emotional responses to the still-face paradigm were investigated in seven-month-old preterm and full-term black infants. Preterm infants spent less time than full-term infants displaying big smiles in episode 1 and a less pronounced decrease in big smiles in episode 2. Maternal depressive symptoms were positively associated with small to medium smiles in the baseline episode but not with big smiles in any episode.

160. Serunian, S.A., & Broman, S.H. (1975). Relationship of Apgar scores and Bayley mental and motor scores. *Child Development, 46,* 696–700.

Infants with Apgar scores of 0 to 3 at one minute had significantly lower eighth-month mental and motor scores than infants with scores of 7 to 10 and significantly lower mental but not motor scores than infants with scores of 4 to 6. Correlations indicated significant relationships (independent of BW) between Apgar scores and BSID scores for random, colored Portuguese, and total samples, but not for blacks and whites.

161. Silverstein, A.B. (1976). Structure of ordinal scales of psychological development in infancy. *Educational & Psychological Measurement, 36,* 355–359.

Intercorrelations among Uzgiris-Hunt scales for two samples of infants were subjected to cluster analysis and factor analysis. One sample was selected so that there were at least four infants at each two months of age between one and two years (mean age, 10 months). The other sample consisted of 51 black 14-month-old firstborns. The results of the procedures were similar for both samples; the three clusters from the first analysis resembled the three factors from the second.

162. Singleton, E.G., Harrell, J.P., & Kelly, L.M. (1986). Racial differentials in the impact of maternal cigarette smoking during pregnancy on fetal development and mortality: Concerns for black psychologists. *Journal of Black Psychology, 12,* 71–83.

Data from six investigations were reevaluated by statistical power analysis to determine if racial differentials existed in the impact of maternal cigarette smoking during pregnancy on LBW and infant mortality. The risk of mortality was significantly greater for infants of black maternal smokers than black nonsmokers, but the same relationship was not evident for whites. The most dramatic increase in mortality was exhibited among infants of black mothers who smoked more than one pack of cigarettes per day.

163. Slesinger, D. (1980). Racial and residential differences in preventive medical care for infants in low-income populations. *Rural Sociology, 45,* 69–90.

Data collected when the infants were 3, 12, and 20 months old were compared on two measures of preventive care: immunization records for DPT, polio, and rubella and frequency of well-child visits. Scores on both measures were highest for urban white infants, followed by urban black infants, then rural white infants. Mother's education, age, number of cases of children, and place of medical service for well-child care were identified as significantly related to the preventive scores.

164. Smith, I.E., Coles, C.D., Lancaster, J., & Fernhoff, P.M. (1986). The effect of volume and duration of prenatal ethanol exposure on neonatal physical and behavioral development. *Neurobehavioral Toxicology & Teratology, 8,* 375–381.

Infants of women who continued to drink throughout pregnancy differed from those of women who did not drink during pregnancy on orientation, autonomic regulation, BW, length, and head circumference. Both infants of women who continued to drink and those of women who stopped showed significant correlations between BW and motor performance. BW of infants in the Continued Drinking group also correlated significantly with abnormal reflexes.

165. Stark, A.D. (1982). Relationship of sociodemographic factors to blood lead concentrations in New Haven children. *Journal of Epidemiology & Community Health, 36,* 133–139.

This study examined blood-lead concentrations (BLCs) in 377 1- to 72-month-old black, white, and Hispanic infants. Characteristics associated with increased BLCs were those that tended to impair the ability of a family to provide the necessary child care and supervision. Risk factors produced different effects on the various race groups.

166. Stephan, C.W., & Langlois, J.H. (1984). Baby beautiful: Adult attributions of infant competence as a function of infant attractiveness. *Child Development, 55,* 576–585.

To determine at what age children first elicit differential expectations from adults as a function of their appearance, a sample of black, Caucasian, and Mexican American adults rated photographs of a sample of black, Caucasian, and Mexican American infants at three time periods in the first year of life. Strong and consistent expectations for the behavior of attractive and unattractive individuals appear to be elicited soon after birth.

167. Stevens, J.H., & Bakeman, R. (1985). A factor analytic study of the HOME scale for infants. *Developmental Psychology, 21,* 1196–1203.

Two factors (Emotional and Verbal Responsivity; Avoidance of Punishment) comprised distinct, independent factors of the HOME scale. Items from three other subscales loaded on a third factor designated Support for Intellectual Development. The HOME's ability to predict intellectual development was most dependent on items reflecting the materials for learning provided by the mother and her instrumental support for developmental advance.

168. Stevens, J.H., & Duffield, B.N. (1986). Age and parenting skill among black women in poverty. *Early Childhood Research Quarterly, 1,* 221–235.

This study examined the relationship between mother's age and maternal behavior reflective of verbal responsivity, punitiveness, and instrumental support for intellectual development in a sample of low-income black women and their infants. Mother's present age was positively correlated with general parenting ability and with verbal responsivity and nonpunitiveness. Among women over 21 years of age, those who became parents while teenagers manifested less optimal parenting and had infants who showed less optimal mental development.

169. Stevens-Simon, C. (1994). Childhood victimization: Relationship to adolescent pregnancy outcome. *Child Abuse & Neglect, 18,* 569–575.

This research studied the pregnancies of poor black 12- to 18-year-olds, some of whom reported that they had been physically or sexually abused prior to conception. Abused adolescents scored significantly higher on stress and depression scales and rated their families as less supportive than did nonabused adolescents. Abused adolescents were more likely to report substance use during pregnancy and gave birth to significantly smaller, less mature infants.

170. Stoiber, K.C., & Anderson, A.J. (1996). Behavioral assessment of coping strategies in young children at-risk, developmentally delayed, and typically developing. *Early Education & Development, 7(1),* 25–42.

The Early Coping Inventory was used to assess coping behaviors in the domains of sensorimotor organization, and reactive and self-initiated behavior. The results suggest that ethnicity accounted for developmental differences found in the at-risk and developmentally delayed groups.

171. Strauss, M.E., Starr, R.H., Ostrea, E.M., Chavez, C.J., & Stryker, J.C. (1977). Behavioral concomitants of prenatal addiction to narcotics. *Annual Progress in Child Psychiatry & Child Development*, 108–118.

Behavioral characteristics of black infants of methadone-treated and nonaddicted mothers were studied during the neonatal period and at 3, 6, and 12 months of age. Several BNBAS measures differentiated between groups. Major differences occurred in irritability of the CNS, and these measures appeared able to predict severity of withdrawal. Mental and motor development was within normal limits in both groups throughout the year. However, the addicted infants showed a progressive decline in psychomotor performance, whereas nonaddicted infants' scores remained stable.

172. Strauss, M.E., Lessen-Firestone, J.K., Starr, R.H., & Ostrea, E.M. (1976). Behavior of narcotics-addicted newborns. *Child Development, 46*, 887–893.

The behavior of black narcotics-addicted and nonaddicted newborns over the first two days of life was assessed with the BNBAS. Addicted infants were less able to be maintained in an alert state and less able to orient to auditory and visual stimuli. These deficits were especially pronounced at 48 hours after birth. Addicted infants were as capable of self-quieting and responding to soothing intervention as normal neonates, although they were substantially more irritable.

173. Sugland, B.W., Zaslow, M.J., Smith, J.R., & Brooks-Gunn, J. (1995). The Early Childhood HOME Inventory and HOME-Short Form in differing racial/ethnic groups: Are there differences in underlying structure, internal consistency of subscales, and patterns of prediction? *Journal of Family Issues, 16*, 632–663.

This study examined differences across European American, African American, and Hispanic American subgroups on the psychometric properties of the Early Childhood HOME Inventory and the HOME-Short Form and the prediction of these two versions to cognitive and socioemotional outcomes among preschool children. Findings suggest few racial/ethnic differences in the psychometric properties of either version of the HOME scale.

174. Suthutvoravut, S., Hogue, C.J., Guyer, B., Anderka, M., & Oberle, M.W. (1989). Are preterm black infants larger than preterm white infants, or are they more misclassified? *Journal of Biosocial Science, 21*, 443–451.

Preterm black infants weighed less than white infants at each gestational age. The proportion of infants less than 2,500 g born at term (greater than or equal to 37 weeks' gestation) was higher (although not significantly) among blacks. These findings are consistent with hypotheses that low SES negatively affects the rate of intrauterine growth.

175. Taylor, G.B., Katz, V.L., & Moos, M.K. (1995). Racial disparity in pregnancy outcomes: Analysis of black and white teenage pregnancies. *Journal of Perinatology, 15*, 480–483.

Results show that pregnant black adolescent women have twice the rate of complications such as prematurity and LBW as those of white teens. The gestational age at the onset of prenatal care and the mean number of prenatal visits were the same for black and white teenagers. No significant differences were found between black and white pregnancies for premature labor, premature delivery, fetal death, neonatal mortality, or hypertensive diseases.

176. Taeusch, H.W., & Supnet, M. (1994). Gestational age, birthweight, and neona-

tal mortality for extremely premature inner-city African-American and Latino infants. *Journal of the National Medical Association, 86,* 297–302.

BW, gestational age, and in-hospital survival for extremely premature infants were examined. Survival rates increased from 15% at 23 weeks gestation to 75% at 28 weeks gestation. Survival in this sample was strongly affected by respiratory distress syndrome, air leak, and BW. Prenatal steroids administered to the mother significantly improved survival in univariate analyses and was at the limits of statistical significance using logistic regression.

177. Underwood, S., Pridham, K., Brown, L., Clark, T., Frazier, W., Limbo, R., Schroeder, M., & Thoyre, S. (1997). Infant feeding practices of low-income African American women in a central city community. *Journal of Community Health Nursing, 14(3),* 189–205.

This article examines the common infant feeding practices of low-income African American women. It also looks at what cultural and economic variables influence infant feeding practices.

178. Vaughn, J., Brown, J., & Carter, J.P. (1986). The effects of maternal anemia on infant behavior. *Journal of the National Medical Association, 78,* 963–968.

This study completed the BNBAS and the BSID for 115 infants whose mothers were predominantly black and from low-income families. Mothers of the more irritable infants had higher iron-binding capacities, whereas the mothers of the less irritable infants had lower iron-binding capacities. Results also reveal that 43% of the mothers had a history of smoking and 55% had a history of coffee consumption.

179. Voight, J.D., Hans, S.L., Bernstein, V.J. (1996). Support networks of adolescent mothers: Effects of parenting experience and behavior. *Infant Mental Health Journal, 17(1),* 58–73.

Larger support networks of adolescents' mothers and friends are associated with better maternal adjustment for adolescent mothers, unless the individuals providing the support were also the individuals providing conflict. The support networks of siblings were related to poorer parenting outcomes.

180. Ward, S.L., Bautista, D., Chan, L., Derry, M., Lisbin, A., Durfee, M.J., Mills, K.S., & Keens, T.G. (1990). Sudden infant death syndrome in infants of substance-abusing mothers. *Journal of Pediatrics, 117,* 876–881.

Infants of substance-abusing mothers (ISAM) were examined to determine whether substance abuse during the perinatal period may be a risk factor for SIDS. The incidence of SIDS was significantly greater in male infants, during the winter months, in black infants, and in non-Hispanic white non-ISAM. Such differences were not observed in the ISAM group. ISAM had a higher incidence of SIDS than the non-ISAM general population. However, it was not possible to separate maternal substance abuse from other confounding variables that may also have had an impact on SIDS risk in the ISAM group.

181. Weaver, J. (1977). Policy responses to complex issues: The case of black infant mortality. *Journal of Health, Politics, Policy and Law, 1,* 433–443.

A considerable body of literature documents the higher infant mortality rate among black Americans. The data for the 1950–1973 period shows that infant mortality is higher for blacks regardless of SES. The roots of higher mortality among blacks may lie in the centuries of nutritional deprivation suffered in America. If true, it is questionable whether traditional social welfare methods will markedly improve the situation. A new set of interventions is needed to reverse the trend toward inequality and injustice that current U.S. infant mortality rates reflect.

182. Whiteside-Mansell, L., & Bradley, R.H. (1996). Early home environment and mental test performance: A structural analysis. *Early Education & Development, 7(3),* 277–295.

A theoretical model of early environment action was examined. The model included SES, cognitive status, and parents' use of negative control. It was found that there were significant associations between SES, early cognitive status, and negative parental control. However, the models for African American and Caucasians differed in structure.

183. Wilson, M.N. (1990). Familial support in the black community. Special Issue: The stresses of parenting. *Journal of Clinical Child Psychology, 19,* 347–355.

This review examines aspects of the black familial network. Infants and young children receive more indirect than direct benefits when their families participate in extended family networks. Single mothers who are active participants in an extended family system have a greater opportunity for self-improvement, work, and peer contact. One dramatic trend is the low availability of marriageable men in the black community. Current socioeconomic difficulties and unstable interpersonal relationships have contributed to the strain on the resources of many black extended family networks.

184. Wise, P., Kotelchuck, M., Wilson, M., & Mills, M. (1985). Racial and socioeconomic disparities in childhood mortality in Boston. *New England Journal of Medicine, 313,* 360–366.

Census data from 1970 and 1980 indicated that childhood mortality was significantly higher among black and low-income children and that black neonatal mortality was elevated at all income levels. Beyond the neonatal period, mortality from respiratory disease, fire, and homicide was related to lower incomes and mortality from motor vehicle injuries was directly related to income. It is concluded that despite Boston residents' high access to tertiary medical care, substantial social differentiation in mortality may exist throughout childhood.

185. Yarrow, L.J., Rubenstein, J.L., Pedersen, F.A., & Jankowski, J.J. (1972). Dimensions of early stimulation and their differential effects on infant development. *Merrill Palmer Quarterly, 18,* 205–218.

A sample of five-month-old black infants (21 boys and 20 girls) who had been cared for by a stable "primary caretaker" were observed in the home. Results show that the natural environment of the young infant can be differentiated into many discrete behaviors of the caretaker, and the properties of objects available to the infant can be subjected to very detailed analyses.

186. Yogman, M.W., Kindlon, D., & Earls, F. (1995). Father involvement and cognitive/behavioral outcomes of preterm infants. *Journal of the American Academy of Child & Adolescent Psychiatry, 34,* 58–66.

This study assessed the effect of father involvement on intellectual and behavioral outcomes of LBW preterm infants followed longitudinally from birth to three years. Most fathers played a meaningful role as play partner with their high-risk infants. Approximately 75% of fathers were reported to play with the baby every day after age 12 months. Fathers who were black, younger, had teenage mothers as companions, or were from low-income families were less involved with their infants. Mean IQ for the high-involvement subgroup was six points higher than for the low-involvement group.

187. Zeskind, P.S. (1983). Cross-cultural differences in maternal perceptions of cries of low- and high-risk infants. *Child Development, 54,* 1119–1128.

The tape-recorded cries of low- and high-risk newborn infants were rated by inner-city Anglo American, black American, and Cuban American mothers during the hospital lying-in period following childbirth. Women rated the cries along four perceptual and six caregiving response scale items. Reliable differences were found between low- and high-risk infant cries on all perceptual responses. The degree of the difference was affected by cultural group differences and and parental experience.

188. Zimmer-Gembeck, M.J., & Helfand, M. (1996). Low birthweight in a public prenatal care program: Behavioral and psychosocial risk factors and psychosocial intervention. *Social Science & Medicine, 43(2)*, 187–197.

Maternal smoking, weight of mother, and rejection of pregnancy were found to be related to an increase of LBW. After controlling for these types of factors, the rate of LBW remained highest for African American mothers.

Asian American Infants

Challenges and Diversity

Domini R. Castellino

A review of the literature over the past 25 years highlights the paucity of research pertaining to Asian American infants. Research focusing on these infants and their families is critical, as the number of Asian American children is increasing substantially in the United States. Currently, approximately one-third of all children in America are children of color, specifically Asian, Hispanic, Native American or African American (Mendoza & Rosales, in press). Between 1980 and 1990, the increase in the Asian American population was 107% (Mendoza & Rosales, 1998). Moreover, these numbers are expected to continue to escalate. By the year 2010, it is estimated that Asian/ Pacific Islanders will constitute 5.6% of all youth between 14 and 24 years of age in the United States (U.S. Bureau of the Census, 1994). Further, projections into the year 2020 indicate that the Asian Pacific population in America will reach approximately 20.2 million.

The accession of Asian Americans in the United States over the past two and a half decades is attributable to both the escalation of American-born Asians, as well as to substantial increases in Asian immigration. In the years preceding 1970, the Asian American population was relatively small. However, the 1965 immigration law opened the door to mass immigration from many countries. For instance, more than 200,000 Asian immigrants have entered the United States annually, over the past two decades, accounting for approximately 45% of the total immigration into this country.

As indicated in Chapter Five of this volume, Asia itself is both culturally and ethnically diverse. However, the term "Asian" is often collectively used to refer to Chinese, Japanese, East Indians, and others, without regard for the specific cultural differences among these groups (McAdoo, 1998). Moreover, intraethnic diversity among particular Asian populations is often overlooked. For example, one of the fastest growing minority populations in the United States, and the largest group of Asian Americans, is the

Chinese. Encompassed within the Chinese American population are individuals of Chinese decent born in America, immigrants from Hong Kong and other countries, as well as refugees from the People's Republic of China and Vietnam (Fong & Browne, 1998). Thus, with many people from different cultures and with different histories, the Chinese American population in and of itself is one of much diversity. For instance, there is the group of Chinese Americans who have been referred to as the "uptown Chinese"; Chinese who fit the stereotypic profile of academic achievers and who typically have brought economic and intellectual resources with them from Asia (Wilson et al.1998). In contrast, there are also many "downtown Chinese" who are socially and economically disadvantaged, often working many hours in semiskilled positions in order to support their families. This latter group of Chinese is in many ways very distinctive from the former group who populate the campuses of Massachusetts Institute of Technology, University of California, Berkeley, and Cornell (Wilson et al., 1998). Moreover, the Census Bureau reports that 21.6 % of Chinese Americans are college graduates and 19.1 % earn a postgraduate or professional degree (Census, 1993). However, almost 17 % of Chinese Americans have less than a ninth grade education. These data alone exemplify the diversity among the Chinese American population with respect to education level and economic resources.

Despite poverty, low parental education, and lack of access to adequate health care among many minority and immigrant groups, the health of minority infants seems to be better than one might expect. The Asian population in particular is no exception. For example, lower rates of low birth weight infants were reported among both foreign-born and American-born Japanese mothers (Alexander, et al., 1996). Lower than expected infant mortality rates have been found among Indochinese refugees from Vietnam, Laos, and Cambodia (Weeks & Rumbaut, 1991). Similarly, Chinese Americans have been reported to have lower fetal, neonatal, and postnatal mortality rates compared to both whites and other ethnic groups (Yu, 1982, 198). However, data on vital statistics have lacked the information necessary to adequately access the possible explanatory factors that may account for these positive outcomes.

Research overall on Asian American infants and their families is lacking considerably. The following citations include only eight studies that have been published between 1965 and 1997. Moreover, research focusing on this population appears to be a very recent phenomenon, given that four out of the eight studies examined were done in the 1990s. Furthermore, over half of the research was comparative in nature and included white infants specifically in their samples.

An analysis of the eight studies yields three distinct themes. Specifically, all of the research focused on parental feeding preferences, infant mortality, or issues related to temperament, day care, and attachment. Based on these investigations, several interesting findings emerged. For example, an examination of feeding practices among Indochinese parents in the United States revealed that these parents prefer formula-feeding to breast-feeding (Fishman, 1988, *191*), and similarly, a sharp decline was observed in breast-feeding of Southeast Asian infants born in the United States as compared to foreign-born Asian infants (Serdula et al., 1991, *195*). Although these two studies alone can hardly be called a trend, they do provide some insight into the feeding decisions made by some Asian parents, and thus, they raise questions regarding the implications of these decisions for infants. The declines in breast-feeding reported in these populations may have an impact on both mother and infant in several ways. For example, bottle-fed infants from poverty-stricken families may be at risk for malnutrition, or at the least undernourishment, due to the expense of bottle-feeding. However, for breast-fed infants, even milk from malnourished mothers will contain the same quality of nutrients as well-nourished mothers (Guthrie, 1979), and therefore, breast-fed infants from these families may fare better. In addition, bottle-fed infants do not receive the immunizing agents that are contained in mothers' milk, which protect against a variety of infections (Jelliffe & Jelliffe, 1988). Thus, many social scientists believe that public health should do more to strengthen the practice of breast-feeding (e.g., Serdula et al., 1991, *195*). Three out of the eight studies in this chapter focused on infant mortality, each from a different perspective. Stahl's (1991, *196*) investigation examined parental *attitudes* toward infant death among Jewish-Oriental parents in particular. The other two studies were comparative in nature, examining the relationship between bed sharing and sudden infant death syndrome (SIDS) (Klonoff-Cohen & Edelstein, 1995, *193*), and the differential mortality rates among white and Chinese American infants (Yu, 1982, *198*).

Three studies assessed more social aspects of infants' development. For example, results have indicated that Chinese working-class children attending day care demonstrate higher cognitive development and less apprehension in unfamiliar settings than those children who do not attend. The children attending day care were also more willing to interact with other unfamiliar children (Kagan, Kearsley & Zelazo, 1977, *192*). Ethnic differences in infant temperament have been found as well. For example, Chinese American infants have been shown to be significantly more withdrawn, less adaptable, and display more negative mood than white infants (Weissbluth, 1982, *197*). However, cultural values, standards, and norms must be taken into account when interpreting these sorts of findings. The differences reported in temperament, for example, may be attributable, at least in part, to differential socialization between white and Chinese American children.

Although the above-noted studies provide some information regarding Asian American infants, much more research needs to be conducted in order to better understand the behavior and development of this population. It is difficult and would, in fact, be inaccurate to draw conclusions or make generalizations regarding the Asian American population based on the very few studies that have been conducted. Moreover, research on a wide variety of topics has not been undertaken at all. For example, no studies were found that addressed issues pertaining to physical and motor development, perceptual development, cognitive issues relating to memory, imitation and habituation, or emotional development. In addition to the necessity for an increase in biopsychosocial research in general, there are several issues that scholars must attend to when conducting research of this nature in the future.

First, data must be collected, interpreted, and reported in such a way that is culturally sensitive. To not do so would pose a serious threat to the validity of such research. For example, comparative studies of academic success among groups of Asian American and white children that do not account for parental socialization for obedience to authority and the high priority placed on academic achievements among Asian families would be neglecting a potentially significant factor relating to the outcome of these investigations. Further, research needs to be conducted in such a way that addresses not only interethnic diversity, but intraethnic diversity as well. Thus, enabling information to be obtained on similarities and differences both between cultures as well as within cultures. It is acknowledged, however, that this line of research is plagued with many difficulties. There are language barriers that exist between researchers and the populations they wish to study. This is true not only among different ethnic groups in general, but within groups as well. For example, within Chinese populations, variations in dialects such as Cantonese and Mandarin further complicate the collection of data on these populations. In addition, Asians tend to be a more "close-mouthed" society, which can make it difficult to recruit and study these populations. Moreover, the methods used to study ethnic populations must also be examined. Methods that have been standardized on white, middle-class American samples pose a threat to the validity of research conducted on infants of color. The history, values, customs, and socioeconomic status of these infants, for example, must all be taken into account.

Further, research on minority infants and children must be mindful about oversampling populations of low socioeconomic status. It is important to assess a wide variety of groups within ethnic populations in order to obtain data that are generalizable to the population being studied (McAdoo, 1998). Since many of the problems of youth in the United States, such as school dropout, violence, and teenage pregnancy, disproportionately affect minority youth (Gibbs, Huang, & Associates, 1989), it is imperative that research be done not only to assess the precursors and implications of such behaviors, but also to better understand what supports, coping abilities, and cultural strengths are available that contribute to the positive outcomes of many minority children (McAdoo, 1998; McLoyd, 1998). Consequently, research on infants that investigates these phenomena are the logical starting point. Moreover, the practice of simply publishing results of research in scientific journals is not adequate any longer. Research must include suggestions for intervention implementation, and results must be translated in such a way as to be understood by advocacy groups, policy designers, and government workers (McAdoo, 1998). The president of the Children's Defense Fund, Marion Wright Edelman (1987), proposes that given the increasing population of racial and ethnic minorities in this country, both the social and economic well-being of the United States in the future will rely more heavily on its capacity to strengthen competencies and positive development, and to decrease negative behaviors and outcomes in all of America's children.

Although Asian American children constitute a smaller number of the American population than some other minority groups, it is still imperative that social science research be conducted on these infants and children in order to better understand their social, emotional, and psychological development and thus, meet the critical needs of all infants and their families in the United States.

REFERENCES

Alexander, G.R., Mor, J.M., Kogan, M.D., Leland, N.L., & Kieffer, E. (1996). Pregnancy outcome of U.S.-born and foreign-born Japanese Americans. *American Journal of Public Health, 86,* 820–824.

Edelman, M.W. (1987). *Families in peril: An agenda for social change.* Cambridge: Harvard University Press.

Fong, R., & Browne, C. (1998). United States immigration policy and Chinese children and families. In H.E. Fitzgerald, B.M. Lester, & B.S. Zuckerman (Eds). *Children of color: Research, health, and policy issues.* (pp. 187–204). New York: Garland.

Gibbs, J.T., Huang, L.N., & Associates. (1989). *Children of color: Psychological interventions with minority youth.* San Francisco: Jossey-Bass.

Guthrie, G.M. (1979). A cross-cultural odyssey: Some personal reflections. In A.J. Marsella, R.G. Tharp, & T.J. Ciborowski (Eds.). *Perspectives on cross-cultural psychology.* New York: Academic Press.

Jelliffe, D.B., & Jelliffe, E.F.P. (1988). Breastfeeding: General review. In D.B. Jelliffe

& E.F.P. Jelliffe (Eds.). *Programmes to promote breastfeeding.* (pp. 3–11). Oxford: Oxford University Press.

McAdoo, H.P. (1998). Diverse children of color: Research and policy implications. In H.E. Fitzgerald, B.M. Lester, & B.S. Zuckerman (Eds.). *Children of color: Research, health, and policy issues.* (pp. 205–218). New York: Garland.

McLoyd, V.C. (1998). Conceptual and methodological issues in the study of ethnic minority children and adolescents. In H.E. Fitzgerald, B.M. Lester, & B.S. Zuckerman (Eds). *Children of color: Research, health, and policy issues.* (pp. 3–24). New York: Garland.

Mendoza, F., & Rosales, N. (1998). The health issues of immigrant children of color. In H.E. Fitzgerald, B.M. Lester, & B.S. Zuckerman (Eds.). *Children of color: Research, health, and policy issues.* (pp. 141–158). New York: Garland.

United States Bureau of the Census, 1993.

United States Bureau of the Census, 1994.

Weeks, J.R., & Rumbaut, R.G. (1991). Infant mortality among ethnic immigrant groups. *Social Science and Medicine, 33,* 327–334.

Wilson, M.N., Pina, L.M., Chan, R., & Soberanis, D.D. (1998). Ethnic minority families and the majority educational system: African American, Chinese American, Hispanic American, and Native American families. In H.E. Fitzgerald, B.M. Lester, & B.S. Zuckerman (Eds.). *Children of color: Research, health, and policy issues.* (pp. 257–280). New York: Garland.

Yu, E. (1982). The low mortality rates of Chinese infants: Some plausible explanations. *Social Science and Medicine, 16,* 253–265.

RESOURCES

189. Baldwin, L.M., & Sutherland, S. (1988). Growth patterns of first-generation Southeast Asian infants. *American Journal of Diseases of Children, 142,* 526–531.

   The median weight, length, and head circumference of 175 healthy, full-term U.S.-born Laotian and Cambodian infants were significantly lower as compared to the values of the National Center for Health Statistics standards for infants older than 6 months. The differences found appeared to be greater for girls than for boys.

190. Bromley, M.A., & Olsen, L.J. (1994). Early intervention services for Southeast Asian children. *Social Work in Education, 16,* 251–256.

   Southeast Asian infants and toddlers took part in the Early Start Project. Children at risk for health, social, and developmental problems were examined in the home. More than 100 families took part in the first two years. Activities that were sensitive to cultural values, customs, norms, and experiences were used. Results indicated that many of the families involved continued to need services. The authors suggest that school service workers examine the influence of Southeast Asian culture on individuals and their families.

191. Fishman, C. (1988). Warm bodies, cool milk: Conflicts in post partum food choice for Indochinese women in California. *Social Science & Medicine, 26(11),* 1125–1132.

   Vietnamese, Cambodian, and ethnic Chinese women ($n = 110$), aged 16–24 and participating in a federal welfare program, were interviewed about their infant feeding decisions and experience. Participants believed that formula was superior to breast milk; one reason involved the Asian humoral medical system. The women hoped to counterbalance excess cooling during childbirth by consuming humorally hot foods for 100 days postpartum. The women preferred using formula for their infants since a hot maternal diet was believed to produce unhealthy breast milk.

192. Kagan, J., Kearsley, R., & Zelazo, P. (1977). The effects of infant day care on psychological development. *Evaluation Quarterly, 1,* 109–142.

Chinese and Caucasian children, some attending a day care center and some staying at home, were assessed at 20 and 29 months. Little difference between day care and non-day care children appeared in cognitive functioning, language use, attachment, protest at separation, or play tempo. Day care children were more willing to interact with unfamiliar other children. Among working-class Chinese children, day care center experience improved cognitive development and reduced apprehension in unfamiliar surroundings, but this pattern did not appear among Caucasians.

193. Klonoff-Cohen, H., & Edelstein, S.L. (1995). Bed sharing and the sudden infant death syndrome. *British Medical Journal, 311(7015)*, 1269–1272.

White, African American, Latin American, and Asian infants who died were compared with 200 living controls to determine whether infants who died of SIDS shared their parents' bed more often than control infants. Although there was a significant difference between bed sharing among African American and Latin American parents compared with white parents, there was no significant relation between routine bed sharing and SIDS.

194. Nakagawa, M., Teti, D.M., & Lamb, M.E. (1992). An ecological study of child-mother attachments among Japanese sojourners in the United States. *Developmental Psychology, 28*, 584–592.

Japanese mothers and their preschoolers who had been living in the U.S. for six months or less reported less social support and more life stress compared to mothers who had been living in the U.S. longer than six months. When life stress was high, mothers indicated they suffered more parenting stress if support was inadequate. High support, especially around marital support, was associated with lower levels of attachment security in children.

195. Serdula, M.K., Cairns, K.A., Williamson, D.F., Fuller, M., & Brown, J.E. (1991). Correlates of breast-feeding in a low-income population of whites, blacks, and Southeast Asians. *Journal of the American Dietetic Association, 91*, 41–45.

Marriage and high parental education were associated with breastfeeding in non-Southeast Asian infants. The initiation of breast-feeding did not appear to be influenced by poverty level, ethnic group, or participation in the Supplemental Food Program for Women, Infants, and Children. The need for public health approaches to strengthen breast-feeding practices is evidenced by the dramatic decline in breast-feeding of Southeast Asian infants who were born in the U.S. as compared to those who were foreign-born.

196. Stahl, A. (1991). Parents' attitudes towards the death of infants in the traditional Jewish-Oriental family. *Journal of Comparative Family Studies, 22*, 75–83.

New children were anxiously awaited in Oriental Jewish families. Through magico-religious practices or modern medicine, when available, families attempted to restore sick children back to health. Since child mortality rates were high, death was met with acceptance and resignation. Consequently, close emotional ties between parents and children were not developed until after the first few dangerous years.

197. Weissbluth, M. (1982). Chinese-American infant temperament and sleep duration: An ethnic comparison. *Journal of Developmental & Behavioral Pediatrics, 3(2)*, 99–102.

Among parents of 23 Chinese American and 60 non-Chinese infants, Chinese American infants were rated as significantly more withdrawing, less adaptable, and more negative in mood as compared to the non-Chinese infants. For the Chinese American infants, longer sleep duration was related to less negative mood. There appear to be ethnic differences in infant temperament with the relationship between negative mood and brief sleep present among different ethnic groups.

198. Yu, E. (1982). The low mortality rates of Chinese infants: Some plausible explanatory factors. *Social Science and Medicine, 16,* 253–265.

A description and interpretation of differential infant mortality rates in white and Chinese Americans are presented. Explanations in the literature for the lower infant mortality among Chinese Americans are reviewed and critiqued. Data from Hong Kong, Taiwan, and mainland China are also reviewed. Finally, research on the fetal consequences and impact of prenatal smoking and drinking on BW in non-Chinese populations is summarized to suggest an alternative explanation for rate differences.

4 LATINO INFANCY RESEARCH

A REFLECTION ON CULTURE AND THE IMPACT OF POVERTY

Carol Barnes Johnson

The infants who are included within the Latino categorization are a diverse and complex group. "Latino" derives from Spanish and is preferred over the English-originated term "Hispanic" by the populace represented by this designation. Hispanic was introduced by the U.S. Bureau of the Census in 1980 to represent those who have a Spanish surname, are born in a Spanish-speaking country, or are Spanish speaking. This classification and its use are often misleading, since the people originating from Mexico, Central and South America, Puerto Rico, and Cuba and other parts of the Caribbean are a heterogeneous group who share a partial heritage and language, while maintaining vastly different cultures and lives. These differences in racial and ethnic populations of Latinos include place of origin, number of years in the United States, immigrant status, levels of acculturation, levels of education, degree of English proficiency and reliance on Spanish language for communication, geographical distribution, and level of economic and political power. Research on infants must reflect this rich heterogeneity.

In 1995 more than 10% of the U.S. population was of Latino origin, which translates into approximately 27 million people (U.S. Bureau of the Census, 1995). Approximately 63% of Latinos originate from Mexico, 13% from Puerto Rico, 12% from Central and South America, 6% from Cuba and 8% from other countries (U.S. Bureau of the Census, 1988). Of these, 40% are foreign-born or were born in Puerto Rico. The Latino population of the United States is quickly rising. In the 10 years before 1990, the Latino population increased by 39%, while during the same period there was an 8% increase in the non-Hispanic white population. By the year 2000, the U.S. Latino population is expected to reach 31 million and make up the largest ethnic group (U.S. Bureau of the Census, 1990). There will be 2.5 million Latino children under 5 years of age, and 6.2 million children in the age range of 5 to 12 years. This increase is due to an increase of immigration into the United States and to high birthrates within the Latino population (COSSMHO, 1993).

Despite this rapid growth there is surprisingly little research centering on Latino infants and their families. Indeed, only 40 articles were found for inclusion in this volume, which encompases the research published from 1970 through 1997. It is encouraging that 25 were published during the time period from 1991 to 1997. The topics of study range from the evaluation of programs designed to overcome cultural barriers in providing care to Hispanic mothers (Bray, 1994, 203), to the influence of the "religiosity" of Mexican American mothers on the development of their infants (Magana, 1995, 222).

Several major themes emerged from the research on Latino infants. First, despite the above described heterogeneity of the Latino community, some studies ignore these differences in people and culture, often categorizing infants included in their studies as Hispanic or Latino. Many researchers argue that to describe the infants within a study by a term that holds little meaning without further clarification jeopardizes the usefulness of the study. Cuellar (1990) states that, "the use of 'Hispanic' without further definition and ethnic qualifiers creates problems for interpretations, applicability of generalizations, and recommendations yielded from one subgroup to another." Similarly, Novello (1991) argues that poorly defined groups result in research, programs and policies not responsive to actual needs and cultures. Many of the studies critiqued were conducted in the early 1980s; it is hoped that as researchers become more informed about the need for the accurate description of the subcultures of the Latino community this lack of specificity will become increasingly less common.

Additionally, the amount of research examining each particular Latino subgroup reflects proportionately their occurrence in the overall population of the United States. A large number of studies focused exclusively on or included infants of Mexican decent (almost one-half), and nine included Puerto Rican infants, four studies incorporated those of Cuban decent, three involved infants from Central and South America, and two included those of Dominican decent.

Another theme that emerged is that much of the research focuses on poorly educated, low income teenage mothers and infants. This is reflective of the conditions of much of the Latino community, as many Latino children continue to live in poverty in the United States. In 1991, the U.S. Bureau of the Census found that 40.4% of Latino children were living under the official poverty line. During the time from 1979 to 1992, Latino families living in poverty increased by 127.2% (Enchautegui, 1995). Nevertheless, over half of Latino children do live above the poverty line. Yet, in only one of the studies was there a comparison of persons identified as lower-class Latino to those identified as middle class. One study described infants born to college-educated parents. The danger here is that study findings to date may be representative of the Latino infant and family living in poverty (as defined by US standards), but may not be indicative of middle- to upper-SES Latino infants.

Despite the one-dimensional perspective evidenced in the choice and description of Latinos in previous research, the topical areas cover a wide range. The major themes include issues of attachment, cognitive development, infant mortality, and the evaluation of various intervention programs. Notably missing are the studies on major areas of development, including language development, motor development, areas of sensory and perceptual abilities, and social development. There are also no studies examining the role of the father in the infant's and mother's lives. This may reflect a general characteristic found in Latino American families, in that the father is seen as having few responsibilities for child rearing, and nurturing is traditionally provided by the mother. The extent to which fathers are or are not directly involved with parenting responsiblities during the 0–3 age period has yet to be determined. Clearly, this is a priority area for future research.

Interestingly, the studies examined for this review overwhelmingly compare samples of Latino infants and mothers to non-Hispanic whites. Further, the comparison often involves infants of low-income Latino families and a more middle-income non-Hispanic white norm, on which our current understanding of infants and their development is largely based. Many studies also complete cross-group comparisons of Latino infants to African American sample groups. Fortunately there are a number of studies that break down the larger Latino/Hispanic classification into more specific infant groups based on country of origin and which conduct cross-group comparisons. One study conducted in Massachusetts examined the association between risk factors and birth weight for Puerto Rican, Dominican, Central American, South American, Mexican, Cuban, and other Latino mothers and infants (Cohen et al., 1993, 208). Another study completed in Florida compared the impact of social networks on infant feeding practices for Cuban, Puerto Rican, and Anglo families (Bryant, 1982, 205).

Overall, a large number of the studies conducted on Latino infants focused on issues that are associated with poverty. This interest skew is observed when noting the amount of studies centering on issues of poor mothers, infant mortality, LBW, malnourishment, poor family support systems, and low socioeconomic status. Knowledge of Latino infants from low-SES families needs to continue to expand, as does research including other economic groups across all of the subgroups of the greater Latino population. There is a need for research focusing on broader aspects of infant development, including cultural factors and their influence on infant development for the many subcultures of the Latino people.

REFERENCES

COSSMHO: The National Coalition of Hispanic Health and Human Service Organizations (1993). *Growing up Hispanic*. Washington, DC: Author.

Cuellar, J. (1990). *Hispanic American aging: Geriatric education curriculum development for selected health professionals*. In *Minority aging: Essential curricula content for selected health and allied health professionals* (DHHS Publication No. HRSPDV 901). Washington, DC: U.S. Department of Health and Human Services.

Enchautegui, M. (1995). *Policy implication of Latino poverty*. Washington, DC: The Urban Institute.

Novello, A. (1991). Hispanic health: time for data, time for action. *Journal of the American Medical Association 265*, 253–255.

U.S. Bureau of the Census, March (1988).

U.S. Bureau of the Census (1990). The Hispanic populations in the United States. Current Population Reports. Series P-20, No. 444. Washington, DC: Government Printing Office.

U.S. Bureau of the Census (1995). March 1994 current population survey, Hispanic data. Washington, DC: U.S. Government Printing Office.

RESOURCES

199. Angel, R. (1988). Single motherhood and children's health. *Journal of Health & Social Behavior, 29*, 38–52.

The effect of a mother's marital status on her report of her child's health for Mexican American, black, and non-Hispanic white children aged 6 months to 11 years was investigated. Single mothers reported poorer overall physical health for their children than did mothers in intact marriages. Mexican American mothers' depression scores were among the most significant predictors of their assessments of their children's health.

200. Arcia, E. (1994). Indicators of developmental and functional status of Mexican-American and Puerto Rican children. *Journal of Developmental & Behavioral Pediatrics, 15*, 27–33.

Indicators of developmental need for special services (LBW, use of NICU, congenital problems, chronic conditions of developmental concern, functional limitations, and physician diagnoses of medical conditions) were examined for Mexican American and Puerto Rican children. Puerto Rican children had substantially poorer status than Mexican American children, who, in turn, had indicators comparable to those reported for the general population.

201. Beckwith, L. (1984). Parent interaction with their preterm infants and later mental development. *Early Child Development & Care, 16*, 27–40.

A study with preterm infants demonstrated that most performed in the normal range on the Gesell Developmental Schedule and the Stanford-Binet Intelligence Scale. However, Hispanic infants and lower-SES Anglo infants showed a performance decrement after nine months. Other findings included gender differences, better performance for firstborns, and the positive effect of mother-infant interactions.

202. Benjamin, G.A., Kahn, M.W., & Sales, B.D. (1984). Developmental differences in infants and policy on undocumented Mexican American parents. *Hispanic Journal of Behavioral Sciences, 6,* 145–160.

Developmental differences between 6- and 18-month-old U.S. infants with undocumented alien parents were assessed. Most of the demographic and environmental variables that could have influenced development were essentially equivalent for both groups. However, undocumented alien infants scored significantly lower on the BMI and BPI. The IBR was strongly associated with cognitive development.

203. Bray, M.L. (1994). A primary health care approach using Hispanic outreach workers as nurse extenders. *Public Health Nursing, 11,* 7–11.

This study examined the effects of a county program for improving the health of Hispanic families, particularly prenatal women and infants. Public health nurses provided assessment, established care plans, evaluated progress, and supervised the workers. Results suggest increased knowledge and positive changes in families' health behaviors. The program also strengthened relationships between the health department and Hispanic families.

204. Bruder, M.B. (1991). Ninos Especiales Program: A culturally sensitive early intervention model. *Journal of Early Intervention, 15,* 268–277.

This study illustrates a home-based program designed to provide culturally sensitive early intervention services to Puerto Rican infants with severe disabilities and their families. Assessments of 15 children and families who were in the program for at least one year show that as family support and informational needs were met, more attention was focused on child intervention needs. An illustrative case study is presented.

205. Bryant, C. (1982). The impact of kin, friend and neighbor networks on infant feeding practices: Cuban, Puerto Rican and Anglo families in Florida. *Social Science and Medicine, 16,* 1757–1765.

This study examines the impact of social networks of Cuban, Puerto Rican, and Anglo families on infant feeding advice and assistance. Influential network members' geographical proximity affected the impact that health care professionals had on mothers' decisions about feeding practices. Network members' advice and encouragement appeared to contribute to a successful lactation experience.

206. Busch-Rossnagel, N.A. (1994). Reliability and validity of a Q-sort measure of attachment security in Hispanic infants. *Hispanic Journal of Behavioral Sciences, 16,* 240–254.

An existing set of items for the Q-sort methodology was adapted for a Hispanic population. Hispanic mothers completed Q-sort ratings, participated in the Strange Situation with their infants, and were visited in their homes. Ratings on the attachment items in the Q-set significantly differentiated Strange Situation attachment classifications.

207. Casal Sosa, A.M., Cobas Selua, M., Damiani Roselli, A., & Fernandez, I. (1986). Estudio del desarrollo psicomotor en 15 ninos desnutridos. Psychomotor development of fifteen undernourished children. *Boletin de Psicologia (Cuba), 9,* 63–79.

This study examined the effects of malnutrition on the psychomotor development of undernourished hospitalized Cuban infants. Nutritional assessment was done using Waterlow's classification based on Harvard standards. Psychomotor development was assessed with the Brunet-Lezine test. A survey of psychosocial factors also was conducted. All studies were done at admission, at discharge upon recovery, and six months later. (In Spanish)

208. Cohen, B.B., Friedman, D.J., Mahan, C.M., Lederman, R., & Munoz, D. (1993). Ethnicity, maternal risk, and birth weight among Hispanics in Massachusetts, 1987–89. *Public Health Reports, 108,* 363–371.

The association between risk factors and BW among Hispanic mothers, classified as Puerto Rican, Dominican, Central American, South American, Mexican, Cuban, and other Hispanic was examined. Substantial variation emerged in mean BW, LBW, and levels of risk among Hispanic subgroups and between Hispanics and white non-Hispanics. Puerto Rican infants had the lowest mean BW and, in general, the highest level of risk factors in this population.

209. Collins, J.W. Jr., & Shay, D.K. (1994). Prevalence of low birth weight among Hispanic infants with United States-born and foreign-born mothers: The effect of urban poverty. *American Journal of Epidemiology, 139,* 184–192.

The investigators examined the contribution of maternal nativity and place of residence to this epidemiologic paradox. The proportion of LBW Hispanic infants ranged from 4.3% for Mexicans to 9.1% for Puerto Ricans. Maternal age, education, trimester of prenatal care initiation, and place of residence were associated with the prevalence of LBW infants among Puerto Rican but not foreign-born Mexican or Central and South American mothers.

210. Eberstein, I., & Pol, L. (1982). Mexican-American ethnicity, socioeconomic status, and infant mortality: A county-level analysis. *Social Science Journal, 19,* 61–71.

Southwestern U.S. counties with a greater proportion of Mexican Americans experienced significantly higher rates of infant mortality. However, when the socioeconomic characteristics of the county populations were controlled, only the relationship between percentage of Mexican American and fetal death ratios remained significant.

211. Engel, T., Alexander, G., & Leland, N. (1995). Pregnancy outcomes of U.S.-born Puerto Ricans: The role of maternal nativity status. *American Journal of Preventive Medicine, 11,* 34–39.

Infants of Puerto Rican (PR)-born and U.S.-born PR mothers had a significantly lower risk of LBW and small-for-gestational-age infants; however, infants of PR-born mothers had a significantly higher risk of neonatal mortality, although they exhibited a significantly lower risk of postneonatal mortality. Infants of PR-born mothers demonstrated higher BW-specific neonatal mortality rates, but lower BW-specific postneonatal mortality rates for nearly every BW category.

212. Fracasso, M.P., Busch-Rossnagel, N.A., & Fisher, C.B. (1994). The relationship of maternal behavior and acculturation to the quality of attachment in Hispanic infants living in New York City. *Hispanic Journal of Behavioral Sciences, 16,* 143–154.

Maternal parenting behavior and patterns of attachment were examined in Puerto Rican and Dominican mother-infant dyads. As in other cross-cultural and subcultural studies, the pattern of attachment classifications differed from that reported for middle-class European American populations. Overall, there was an equal number of secure and insecure infants. Sex differences were revealed in the distribution of attachment patterns.

213. Fuentes-Afflick, E., & Lurie, P. (1997). Low birth weight and Latino ethnicity: Examining the epidemiologic paradox. *Archives Pediatrics and Adolescent Medicine, 151(7),* 665–674.

This article looks at the relation between Latino ethnicity, Latino subgroup, and LBW. LBW rates of Latinos and whites are similar. However, among Latinos, Puerto Ricans have higher LBW rates.

214. Gonzales, M.D., Montgomery, G., Fucci, D., Randolph, E., & Mata-Pistokache, T. (1997). A comparison of language abilities between two groups of premature Hispanic infants and one group. *Infant Toddler Intervention: The Transdisciplinary, 7(1)* 1–16.

The receptive and expressive language development of LBW premature, higher birth weight premature, and full-term Mexican American infants was explored. The results suggest that LBW premature infants are at greater risk than higher birth weight premature infants for speech and language delays.

215. Goss, G.L., Lee, K., Koshar, J., Heilemann, M.S., & Stinson, J. (1997). More does not mean better: Prenatal visits and pregnancy outcome in the Hispanic population. *Public Health Nursing, 14(3)*, 183–188.

A comparative study was conducted to examine the number of prenatal visits and the outcomes of Mexico-born Hispanics and U.S.-born Hispanics. The results show that more prenatal visits did not improve the outcome during pregnancy, labor, or the postpartum period.

216. Guendelman, S., English, P., & Chavez, G. (1995). The effects of maternal health behaviors and other risk factors on immunization status among Mexican-American infants. *Pediatrics, 95*, 823–828.

This study investigated Latino mother-infant pairs to determine whether maternal health risk behaviors are associated with infant immunization status. When grouped together in a maternal health risk index, maternal health behaviors showed a dose-response relationship with inadequate immunization status. Marital status, parity, life stress, time lived in neighborhood, Spanish language, and child age were also important predictors.

217. Harwood, R.L. (1992). The influence of culturally derived values on Anglo and Puerto Rican mothers' perceptions of attachment behavior. *Child Development, 63*, 822–839.

This study examined indigenous concepts of desirable and undesirable attachment behavior among middle- and lower-class Anglo and lower-class Puerto Rican mothers to formulate culturally sensitive criteria of normative attachment behavior. The Anglo mothers focused more on characteristics associated with the presence or absence of individual autonomy. The Puerto Rican mothers placed more emphasis on the child's ability to maintain proper demeanor in a public context.

218. Hedderson, J., & Daudistel, H. (1982). Infant mortality of the Spanish surname population. *Social Science Journal, 19*, 67–78.

An examination of infant mortality rates for the Spanish surname population in El Paso County, Texas, was based on health department statistics for the years 1970–1971 and 1975–1978. The data do not support the hypothesis that the Spanish surname infant mortality rate is substantially biased downward because of underregistration.

219. John, A.M., & Martorell, R. (1989). Incidence and duration of breast-feeding in Mexican-American infants, 1970–1982. *American Journal of Clinical Nutrition, 50*, 868–874.

Children born into households with a college-educated head were shown to be more likely to be breast-fed than were other children; breast-feeding was also positively associated with BW. Infants in households for which the preferred interview language was Spanish were more likely to be breast-fed than were infants living in households for which the interview was conducted in English.

220. Johnson, D.L., & Breckenridge, J.N. (1982). The Houston Parent-Child Development Center and the primary prevention of behavior problems in young children. *American Journal of Community Psychology, 10,* 305–316.

The effectiveness of the Houston Parent-Child Development Center (PCDC), a two-year, intensive parent-child education program for one- to three-year-old children with low-income Mexican-American families was evaluated. The principal result is that boys in the control group were more destructive, overactive, negative, attention-seeking, and less emotionally sensitive than program boys and girls from both groups.

221. Leyendecker, B. (1995). The social worlds of 8- and 12-month-old infants: Early experiences in two subcultural contexts. *Social Development, 4,* 194–208.

This study compared the everyday experiences of infants from families who migrated recently from Central America to the U.S. and from middle-class European American families. Experiences and activities were very similar in both groups, and the effects of the mothers', fathers', or others' presence on ongoing activities were also similar. The groups differed with regard to the circadian distribution of activities, opportunities for interactions with various people, and the differences between weekdays and weekends.

222. Magana, A. (1995). Examining a paradox: Does religiosity contribute to positive birth outcomes in Mexican American populations? *Health Education Quarterly, 22,* 96–109.

Mexican American women, despite their relatively lower SES, deliver significantly fewer LBW babies and lose fewer babies to all causes during infancy than do women of other ethnic groups. It is suggested that lack of research on cultural similarities and differences in Hispanic/Latino subgroups has led to faulty or simplistic understanding on health behavior and status.

223. McGowan, R.J., Johnson, D.L., & Maxwell, S.E. (1981). Relations between infant behavior ratings and concurrent and subsequent mental test scores. *Developmental Psychology, 17,* 542–553.

Lower-SES Mexican American infants (n = 125) were administered the BSID and the Stanford-Binet Intelligence Scale. Results indicate that neither the factor scores from the principal components analysis nor the composite scores for Primary Cognition and Extraversion added significantly to the prediction of subsequent mental performance beyond what was afforded by 12-month BMI scores.

224. McKenna, J., Mosko, S., Richard, C., & Drummond, S. (1994). Experimental studies of infant-parent co-sleeping: Mutual physiology and behavioral influences and their relevance to SIDS (sudden infant death syndrome). *Early Human Development, 38,* 187–201.

The possibility that sensory exchanges during mother-infant cosleeping alter infants' sleep experiences and may help them resist some kinds of SIDS was evaluated. Infants who sleep with their mothers and breast-feed are more likely to sleep on their backs, are aroused by their mothers at unexpected moments, breathe in small amounts of their mother's CO_2, experience increased movement and feeding, and consequently exhibit greater vagal tone maturity.

225. Montgomery, G., Fucci, D., Gonzales, M.D., Bettagere, R., Reynolds, M.E., & Petrosino, L. (1995). Effects of prematurity on the language development of Hispanic infants. *Infant-Toddler Intervention: The Transdisciplinary Journal, 5,* 219–231.

Language development at age 22 months was compared in a sample of 12 premature and 12 full-term Mexican American infants using the Sequenced Inventory of Communication Development-Revised. Findings indicate that in Mexican American premature infants, language acquisition may occur more slowly than for full-term infants. In addition, expressive language skills appear to be more affected than receptive language skills.

226. Moore, P., Fenlon, N., & Hepworth, J.T. (1996). Indicators of differences in immunization rates of Mexican American and white non-Hispanic infants in a Medicaid managed care system. *Public Health Nursing, 13,* 21–30.

Immunization levels of Mexican American and white non-Hispanic infants enrolled in Arizona's Medicaid managed care demonstration project, a prototype of the model proposed for a reformed health care system, were compared. Significant predictors of a higher number of immunizations included fewer siblings, older maternal age, and higher maternal education. Health insurance and enrollment in a managed care plan were not sufficient to ensure adequate immunization of Medicaid-enrolled infants.

227. Moore, P., & Hepworth, J.T. (1994). Use of perinatal and infant health services by Mexican American Medicaid enrollees. *Journal of the American Medical Association, 272,* 297–304.

Characteristics associated with use of health services for Mexican American women were explored. Mexican Americans averaged fewer prenatal visits than non-Hispanic whites and were less likely to have adequate prenatal care, but both groups of mothers were well below the 68% of women nationally who receive adequate prenatal care. Even after controlling for SES and cultural characteristics, ethnicity had a strong independent effect on the number of prenatal visits and adequacy of prenatal care.

228. Mosko, S., Richard, C., McKenna, J., & Drummond, S. (1996). Infant sleep architecture during bedsharing and possible implications for SIDS. *Sleep, 19(9),* 677–684.

All-night laboratory polysomnographic recordings were performed in Latino infants within the peak age range for SIDS, in both bed-sharing (with mother) and solitary sleeping environments. The results suggest that accepted normative values for infant sleep established in solitary sleeping infants may not be representative of infants raised in social sleeping environments.

229. Pena, I.C. (1987). The Gesell Developmental Schedule in Hispanic low-birth weight infants during the first year of life. *Infant Behavior & Development, 10,* 199–216.

The Gesell Developmental Schedule (GDS) was adminstered to LBW, high-risk Hispanic infants to determine whether this test is appropriate for this population. The GDS appeared to be a useful developmental test for this population; values for the overall developmental quotient did not deviate from the GDS norms. Slight deviations from the norm in gross motor, fine motor, and language subscales were observed at 40 weeks corrected chronological age. BW and small-for-gestational-age categories influenced the outcome.

230. Rogers, R. (1984). Infant mortality among New Mexican Hispanics, Anglos, and Indians. *Social Science Quarterly, 65,* 876–884.

Endogenous, exogenous, and total aggregate infant mortality rates were compared among Hispanics, Anglos, and Indians. The cause-specific rates show whether ethnic groups are differentially affected by environmental causes or inborn causes. Hispanic and Anglo rates are equivalent, but Indian rates of exogenous and total aggregate infant mortality are statistically higher than for either Anglos or Hispanics.

231. Ruiz, P. (1985). Cultural barriers to effective medical care among Hispanic-American patients. *Annual Review of Medicine, 36,* 63–71.

Cultural barriers to the effective medical management of Cubans, Puerto Ricans, and Mexican Americans were explored. A culturally related syndrome of Puerto Ricans is described, which involves trembling, seizurelike convulsions, and semi-consciousness with no physical pathology. Culture functions as a barrier to medical management in its view of illness as supernaturally related.

232. Sherraden, M.S., & Barrera, R.E. (1996). Poverty, family support, and well-being of infants: Mexican immigrant women and childbearing. *Journal of Sociology and Social Welfare, 23(2),* 27–54.

Interviews with 41 women revealed that family support plays an important role in reducing LBW births in the Mexican immigrant population. However, family support does not seem to a protective factor for women living in extreme poverty.

233. Sontag, J.C. (1994). An ethnic comparison of parent participation and information needs in early intervention. *Exceptional Children, 60,* 422–433.

This study investigated ethnic differences in parents' perceptions of their information needs and sources of information, and the nature of parent participation in early intervention and participation preferences. Parents reported a high degree of involvement in meeting their children's service needs.

234. Teberg, A.J., Howell, V.V., & Wingert, W.A. (1983). Attachment interaction behavior between young teenage mothers and their infants. *Journal of Adolescent Health Care, 4,* 61–66.

Behavioral interactions between low-SES Hispanic teenage mothers and their infants and an older control group of mothers and infants were compared. Infant attachment, exploration, and stress-adaptation behaviors, and maternal ability to contact, encourage, and comfort the infant were evaluated. Control mothers differed significantly from teenage mothers in effective eye, verbal, and physical contact, and smiling behaviors.

235. Trevathan, W.R. (1988). First conversations: Verbal content of mother-newborn interaction. *Journal of Cross-Cultural Psychology, 19,* 65–77.

The conversations of Hispanic and Anglo mothers during interactions with their newborn infants in the first 10 minutes after birth were recorded. Analysis of verbal content revealed that comments about the infant's resemblance to family members were rare. Questions or comments about the infant's gender were far more frequent than in previous studies.

236. Walker, D.S., & Koniak-Griffin, D. (1997). Evaluation of a reduced-frequency prenatal visit schedule for low-risk women at a free-standing birthing center. *Journal of Nurse Midwifery, 42(4),* 295–303.

This article examines the effectiveness of a reduced-frequency prenatal visit schedule for low risk pregnant women. Women who followed the reduced-frequency visit schedule experienced no difference in perinatal outcomes or anxiety when compared to women who followed a regular prenatal visit schedule.

237. Wolff, C.B., & Portis, M. (1996). Smoking, acculturation, and pregnancy outcome among Mexican Americans. *Health Care for Women International, 17(6),* 563–573.

The article examines the role of acculturation in smoking practices and pregnancy outcome of Mexican American women. Among the more acculturated women, the prevalence of smoking and poor birth outcomes did not increase, and the women at the moderate level of acculturation appear to have the greatest need for public health services rather than women with the lowest level of acculturation.

238. Wolff, C., Portis, M., & Wolff, H. (1993). Birth weight and smoking practices during pregnancy among Mexican-American women. *Health Care for Women International, 14,* 271–279.

Smoking practices during pregnancy and the effects of smoking on BW were examined using data from the 1983–1984 Hispanic Health and Nutrition Examination Survey of 549 Mexican-American mothers and 778 births in the southwestern U.S. Approximately 25% of the mothers had smoked during pregnancy, and infants born to these women weighed significantly less at birth than did those whose mothers had not smoked; for each cigarette per day, birth weight decreased by 7.4 g.

NATIVE AMERICAN AND ALASKAN ALUET INFANCY RESEARCH

A DISADVANTAGED CULTURE

Mary Judge-Lawton

The literature search for information about Native American and Alaskan Aleut infants and their families uncovered only 24 articles about the Native American population. Currently, the U.S. government recognizes that Native Americans have a disproportionately low socioeconomic status and has a long history of funded programs designed to enhance education and health. However, the history between the U.S. government and Native Americans is fraught with tension. The "Indian Unit" as taught in schools illustrates a continuing misrepresentation and apathy toward Native Americans. The taking of land, forced relocation, an institutionally racist educational system, removal of Indian children from their homes, U.S. paternalism, breaking of multiple treaties, obstacles to self-governance, and stripping of tribal recognition and denial of religious freedom are all remembered in the lives of the Native Americans. Overall, the Native Nation believes that federal policy is equal to Native American genocide.

Cited over and over are such issues as: tribal sovereignty, Indian identity, civil rights, economic development, gaming, alcoholism, and the continuing argument over sacred lands. Directly or indirectly, these issues affect the health and welfare of the Native American infant and his or her family.

The Native Nations have had ongoing disagreement with the U.S. government regarding the rights of the tribes to be a sovereign nation. Where the government has said that Native Americans have rights under the U.S. constitution, and have enacted the Civil Rights Act (1968) and the Indian Child Welfare Act (1978), among others, the Native Americans will say that no Native Nation ever ratified the U.S. Constitution. They state that they are not a part of the U.S. or its federal system.

The Indian Child Welfare Act of 1978 was supposed to be an affirmation of the value of Indian cultures, their ability to self-perpetuate and enculturate their children into a tribal belief and value system. Unfortunately, the act illustrates extreme value differences, including different styles of parenting, tribal systems, and values of the individual and the family. The government designing an Act for the Indians is made more difficult because each tribe is run differently, and each has its own issues. To the credit of the U.S. government, one part of this three-part act is for Indian child and family program development, and Indian associations have stated that the act has made a difference. However, they acknowledge that tribal problems still persist and that there is inadequate funding at tribal and state levels.

A more recent problem is the question of exactly who qualifies as a Native American. This question has caused disagreements within tribes as well as between governmental authorities. The federal definitions are confusing and can result in, for example, a Native American receiving an educational benefit, but not a medical benefit. In the 1990 census, there were 1.8 million self-proclaimed Indians in the U.S. The Bureau of Indian Affairs' Branch of Acknowledgment and Recognition believes that not only has there been much interracial breeding, there are many who wish to say they are Indian, just for the sake of saying they are Indian. It is estimated that a half million ethnic Indians receive no federal benefits because they do not happen to be members of a federally recognized tribe.

Civil rights were addressed in 1968 when the Indian Civil Rights bill was enacted to ensure that all American "freedoms" were extended to all Native Americans. However, there was no money appropriated for its enforcement; consequently, after years of tribal complaints not being recognized, the complaints diminished. In 1991, the U.S. Commission on Civil Rights stated that it had no money appropriated for the enforcement of Native American civil rights.

Prior to 1975, the economic development of the Native American Tribes was directed by the U.S. government. In 1975, the Tribes became in charge of industry that was previously run by the Bureau of Indian Affairs. Currently, tribal gaming has become a $6 billion industry. Money has been used within these tribes for everything from housing and college scholarships to sewer systems and health clinics.

Despite the economic developments, alcoholism remains a catastrophic tribal problem. According to the Indian Health Service, Indians are three and a half times more likely than other Americans to die from cirrhosis of the liver, four times more likely to die from alcohol-related accidents, and three times more likely to die from alcohol-related homicide or suicide. Between 5% and 25% of infants may be mentally or physically damaged by fetal alcohol syndrome, and alcohol is responsible for many other social problems.

Economically speaking, Native Americans have the lowest average income and the highest proportion of families below the official poverty line. Native Americans have a lower medial income than either African Americans or white Americans. The median income of Native Americans living on reservations is one-third of the median white income. These figures illustrate failure of policies that intervene, to help the uneven distribution of wealth, which leaves the Native American children and their families at risk for a lesser standard of health and welfare.

The topics given the greatest amount of consideration in the search for information related to infants and their families were child development issues and both physical health and mental health. The most common theme was that Native American culture is a disadvantaged culture especially within the issue of infant health. Studies cite lack of prenatal care, increased infant mortality and morbidity, less than standard cognitive development, lack of parent training opportunities, increased risks for child abuse and neglect, and alcohol abuse.

Articles covered a wide range of topics: Two articles concerned pregnant adolescents and their deliveries (Buck et al., 1992, 243; Liu, 1994, 252), several articles studied birth weights and infant outcomes (Buck et al., 1992, 243; VanLandingham & Hogue, 1995, 261), and several studies focused on sudden infant death syndrome (Burd, 1994, 244; Irwin, Mannino & Daling, 1992, 251), language development (Mayfield 1985, 226; McShane, 1988, 255), and sleep (Burd, 1994, 244). One article studied dental caries (Tsubouchi et al., 1995, 260), and there was an anthropological study describing how a tribe viewed early childhood and death (Moffat, 1994, 256). Other studies encompassed many of the above issues plus abuse and neglect, obesity, other health issues, and alcohol use (Berlin, 1987, 241; Broussard et al., 1995, 242; DeBruyn, 1992, 246; May, 1988, 253; McShane, 1988, 255; Spivey, 1977, 259). Several studies contrasted breast-feeding and bottle-feeding (Ellestad-Sayed et al, 1979, 248; May, 1988, 253), and one correlated the method of feeding with the amount of times the infants were seen for infection related illness (Ellestad-Sayed, 1979, 248). Cultural differences were highlighted in studies measuring the reliability of standardized tools in the Native American culture (Seideman, 1992, 257; Seideman et al., 1994, 258).

The studies that discussed the use of tools for assessment of infant attachment (the Strange Situation), home assessments (the Caldwell HOME Inventory), and the Nursing Child Assessment Teaching Scale show that there are cultural differences that need to be considered before using these tools (Seideman, 1992, 257; Seideman et al., 1994, 258). Even the studies considering motor development revealed that cultural differences are considerable in the early development of infants (Chisholm, 1978, *245;* Dennis, 1991, *247;* Harriman, 1982, *250;* McShane, 1988, *255;* Spivey, 1977, *259*).

Several studies researched birth weights and mortality/morbidity issues (Burd, 1994, *244;* Irwin, Mannino & Daling, 1992, *251;* VanLandingham & Hogue, 1995, *261*). The related health issues are discussed with general indications that Native American infants are at a disadvantage starting with their prenatal care because the pregnant teens studied waited longer to begin their prenatal care (Buck et al., 1992, *243;* Liu, 1994, *252*). After birth and throughout infancy, the babies are at a disadvantage when it comes to well-baby care and birth-weight issues (Buck et al., 1992, *243;* Liu, 1994, *252;* May, 1988, *253*). Continued culturally based research is needed in order to increase our knowledge about the development of the Native American infant.

If culture is the way members of a population look through their lens to see the world around them, then use this lens to interpret events, to moderate their behavior, and to react to their reality, those involved with care and research of the Native American then must look through the Native American lens. Government and research can invest in Native American concerns regarding their rights, and helping the Native Americans increase their economic status. Simultaneously, research can focus on understanding the development of the Native American infant, and sharing the information with the Native Americans so that they may acquire the knowledge needed to increase their health status. Ultimately, the Native Nation families can become healthier within the context of their culture.

RESOURCES

239. Adams, M., MacLean, C., Niswander, J. (1968). Discrimination between deviant and ordinary low birth weight: American Indian infants. *Growth, 32,* 153–161.

240. Bauer, M., & Wright, A. (1996). Integrating qualitative and quantitative methods to model infant feeding behavior among Navajo mothers. *Human Organization, 55(2),* 183–192.
    The investigators use both qualitative and quantitative methods to create a decision model of the choice of breast-feeding or formula-feeding. The model accurately predicted the initial infant feeding behavior for 96% of the sample.

241. Berlin, I. (1987). Effects of changing native American cultures on child development. *Journal of Community Psychology, 15,* 299–306.
    Child abuse and neglect, substance abuse, depression, and poor school learning are critical developmental issues for children on many Native American reservations. The efforts of a few American Indian communities to emphasize the teaching of traditional ways and to deal with community problems in new ways are described.

242. Broussard, B.A., Sugarman, J.R., Bachman-Carter, K., Booth, K., Stephenson, L.,

Strauss, K., & Gohdes, D. (1995). Toward comprehensive obesity prevention programs in Native American communities. *Obesity Research, 2,* 289–297.

The challenge of obesity in the Native American is manifest in the increasing rates of non-insulin-dependent diabetes mellitus. Studies of Native American infants, children, and adults have confirmed a high prevalence of overweight. Because of the cultural diversity among Native Americans, future studies should focus on collecting community- and region-specific data and should emphasize the need for obesity prevention through culturally appropriate community- and school-based behavioral interventions.

243. Buck, G.M., Mahoney, M.C., Michalek, A.M., Powell, E.J., & Shelton, J.A. (1992). Comparison of Native American births in upstate New York with other race births, 1980–1986. *Public Health Reports, 107,* 569–575.

Birth records of New York neonates indicated that mothers of Native American and black infants were more likely to be younger, have a higher parity, be of lower educational attainment, and have delayed initiation of prenatal care than mothers of white or other-race infants. Native American infants were similar to white and other-race infants in rates of LBW and premature birth. Black infants were twice as likely as the other three groups of infants to be LBW or premature.

244. Burd, L. (1994). Prevalence of prone sleeping position and selected infant care practices of North Dakota infants: A comparison of whites and Native Americans. *Public Health Reports, 109,* 446–449.

Chippewa, Sioux, Hidasta, Arikara, and Mandan mothers reported that 69% of their infants slept prone, 17% slept supine, and 14% slept on their side. Native American infants were 3.2 times more likely to die from SIDS compared to other North Dakota infants. These Native American infants slept prone 46.9% of the time compared with 74.4% of white infants.

245. Chisholm, J.S. (1978). Swaddling, cradleboards and the development of children. *Early Human Development, 2(3),* 255–275.

Results of an ethological study of cradleboard use among Navajo Indians indicated that time on the cradleboard declined from about 16 hours per day in the first 3 months to less than 9 hours by the first birthday. It is suggested that swaddling and cradleboard might reduce the social isolation of infants as well as parent-child tension associated with babies who have sleeping problems.

246. DeBruyn, L. (1992). A comparative study of abused and neglected American Indian children in the Southwest. *Social Science & Medicine, 3(5),* 305–315.

This study compared descriptive, qualitative, and quantitative data from a clinically identified sample of abused and neglected Indian children with a matched sample of controls. Alcohol abuse was present in virtually all families that abused or neglected their children; however, alcohol abuse existed exclusive of the association with child abuse/neglect. Results suggest that alcohol abuse is a necessary, but not sufficient, condition for child abuse/neglect.

247. Dennis, W. (1991). The effect of cradling practices upon the onset of walking in Hopi children. Special Issue: Centennial Issue. *Journal of Genetic Psychology, 152,* 563–572.

In all but two Hopi Indian villages in Arizona, infants were tightly bound to a cradling board on the first day of life, and for the first three months could move only the head. Thereafter, the amount of freedom increased gradually, with great individual differences in the age at which the board is discarded (range for 14 cases: 4 to 14 months). There were no statistically significant differences in age at onset of walking. (Originally published in 1940.)

248. Ellestad-Sayed, J., Coodin, F.J., Dilling, L.A., Haworth, J.C. (1979). Breast-feeding protects against infection in Indian infants. *Canadian Medical Association Journal, 120,* 295–298.

A retrospective study was conducted in two isolated Manitoba Indian communities to determine whether type of infant feeding was related to infection during the first year of life. Breast-feeding was protective against severe infection requiring hospital admission, as well as against minor infection. Fully bottle-fed infants were hospitalized with infectious diseases 10 times more often and spent 10 times more days in the hospital during the first year of life than fully breast-fed infants.

249. Evers, S., & Rand, C. (1982). Morbidity in Canadian Indian and non-Indian children in the first year of life. *Canadian Medical Association Journal, 126,* 249–252.

The patterns of morbidity in the first year of life for Indian and non-Indian infants living in southern Ontario were studied. Among Indians, the rate of hospital admission was 4 times greater and the risk of illness of most diagnostic categories was more than 1.5 times greater than that of non-Indians. There were no differences in the rates of visits to hospital emergency rooms. Only 36% of the Indian infants attended five or more well-baby examinations compared to 68% of the non-Indian infants.

250. Harriman, A. (1982). On why Wayne Dennis found Hopi infants retarded in age at onset of walking. *Perceptual & Motor Skills, 55,* 79–86.

The present study supplemented the interview procedure used by Dennis (1940) with questions concerning circumstances of Hopi life that may have been responsible for the retardation. Results show that contemporary Hopi infants, who began walking at a mean age of 12.5 months, were advanced by 2.5 months over the date of walking recorded by Dennis. Infants reared on the cradleboard, like those studied by Dennis, walked as early as unrestrained infants.

251. Irwin, K.L., Mannino, S., & Daling, J. (1992). Sudden infant death syndrome in Washington State: Why are Native American infants at greater risk than white infants? *Journal of Pediatrics, 121,* 242–247.

Native Americans are over three times more likely than white infants to die of SIDS. A population-based retrospective cohort study indicated that the risk for SIDS diminished after adjustment for differences between Native American and white mothers in age, marital status, parity, and smoking status during pregnancy.

252. Liu, L.L. (1994). Pregnancy among American Indian adolescents: Reactions and prenatal care. *Journal of Adolescent Health, 15,* 336–341.

The reactions and prenatal care of 20 American Indian adolescents were explored. Five teens received adequate prenatal care, 13 received intermediate prenatal care, and 2 received inadequate prenatal care. During the pregnancy, 3 women used tobacco, 3 used alcohol; none admitted to other drugs. Although only 1 teen planned the pregnancy, 15 were not using contraception when they became pregnant. Most were afraid to tell their families and 4 concealed the pregnancy until confronted. During the pregnancy, 7 adolescents described loneliness and 6 expressed suicidal ideation.

253. May, P. (1988). The health status of Indian children: Problems and prevention in early life. *American Indian & Alaska Native Mental Health Research.* Monograph 1, 244–283.

Data on death and disease patterns of American Indian and Alaska native children were reviewed. It was concluded that major reductions in the current high rates of morbidity and mortality can be implemented through prenatal care; cessation of prenatal alcohol consumption; a safer, hygienic environment for infants and youth; increased breast-feeding of infants to six to eight months of age; informed use of baby bottle-feeding; and the use of car seats and other protective devices for infants.

254. Mayfield, M.I., & Davies, G. (1984). An early intervention program for native Indian infants and their families. *Canadian Journal of Public Health, 75,* 450–453.

A program is descibed that was adopted by 5 native Indian bands in British Columbia in which parents promote their children's early language and reading skills in the home. An evaluation using the Denver Developmental Screening Test and interviews with parents and local professionals supported the usefulness of the program. Key factors in planning and implementing such programs are identified.

255. McShane, D. (1988). An analysis of mental health research with American Indian youth. Special Issue: Mental health research and service issues for minority youth. *Journal of Adolescence, 11,* 87–116.

The literature was reviewed on mental health research conducted with American Indian infants, children, and adolescents since 1970. Specific areas addressed include otitis media, fetal alcohol syndrome, abuse and neglect, failure to thrive, autism, enuresis during early development, neurosensory disorders, developmental disabilities, handicapping conditions, school-related problems, foster care and adoption, self-concept/identity, conduct disorders/delinquency, drug and alcohol use, and suicide and depression for school-aged children and adolescents.

256. Moffat, T. (1994). Infant mortality and cultural concepts of infancy: A case study from an early twentieth century aboriginal community. Special Issue: The anthropology of infancy. *Pre- & Peri-Natal Psychology Journal, 8,* 259–273

This study explores the impact of infant death on cultural perceptions of infancy, using data from a study of infant mortality in a Canadian aboriginal Cree-Ojibwa community during the period 1910–1939. A very high overall rate of 249 infant deaths per 1,000 live births was recorded for this period. It is suggested that high infant mortality contributed to a delay in the point at which personhood was conferred on the infant. Differing cultural perceptions surrounding infant death provided the Canadian government with a rationale to contest aboriginal autonomy over child welfare.

257. Seideman, R.Y. (1992). Using NCAST instruments with urban American Indians. *Western Journal of Nursing Research, 14,* 308–319.

This study evaluated the appropriateness of the Nursing Child Assessment Satellite Training (NCAST) for use among urban American Indians (AIs). Thirty-five AI children (aged 1 month to 3 years) and their mothers participated in the study. The NCAST tools reflected urban AI parenting practices and could probably be used to identify potentially problematic AI parenting situations. Results demonstrate the heterogeneous nature of the AI population in the contemporary urban setting and the need for complexity in approaches to understanding the AI family and parenting practices.

258. Seideman, R., Williams, R., Burns, P., & Jacobson, S. (1994). Culture sensitivity in assessing urban Native American parenting. *Public Health Nursing, 11,* 98–103.

This study explored the effectiveness of using the HOME and the Nursing Child Assessment Teaching Scale (NCATS) with 63 urban Native American mothers and their children (aged 3 months to 3 years). Relative to the instruments' norms, scores were lower on the play and involvement subscales of the HOME and higher on the total parent, clarity of cues, response to parent, and total child subscales of the NCATS. Analyses support the usefulness of these instruments with Native American parents.

259. Spivey, G. (1977). The health of American Indian children in multi-problem families. *Social Science & Medicine, 11,* 357–359.

The author compared medical chart histories of American Indian children from 10 families with multiple psychosocial problems with those of children from 10 adequately functioning families living in similar conditions on reservations. Distinct differences were found for the first year of life, with children of multiproblem families having more illness and less well-baby care than children of control families. It is concluded that children of multiproblem families will benefit from special medical and social services, particularly those that will improve their general socioeconomic and environmental conditions.

260. Tsubouchi, J., Tsubouchi, M., Maynard, R.J., Domoto, P.K., Weinstein, P. (1995). A study of dental caries and risk factors among Native American infants. *ASDC Journal of Dentistry for Children, 62,* 283–287.

A sample of 77 infants, ages 12 to 36 months, were examined in a Women Infant Children (WIC) program at a health center in Washington. Questionnaires were completed regarding children's feeding, general care, and dental health behavior, and dental examinations were conducted. Caries in children was significantly associated with bottle-feeding, giving a bottle as the baby falls sleep, and snacks between meals. Brushing behavior was also related to caries. These results suggest feeding patterns beyond bottle use appear to be behavioral risk factors in the prevalence of infant caries in this population.

261. VanLandingham, M., & Hogue, C. (1995). Birthweight-specific infant mortality risks for Native Americans and whites, United States, 1960 and 1984. *Social Biology, 42,* 83–94.

The National Center for Health Statistics 1960 and 1984 natality and linked-birth/death certificate tapes were used to compare BW-specific neonatal and postneonatal mortality risks for Native Americans and whites. Improvements for Native Americans were highest in postneonatal survival. BW was positively associated with survival for both groups. Improvements in neonatal mortality for both groups were highest at the lower BWs, whereas the gains in postneonatal survival were most beneficial to normal and high BW infants.

PART 2
CENTRAL AND SOUTH AMERICA

6 LATIN AMERICAN INFANTS

RESEARCH ON POVERTY, POVERTY IN RESEARCH

Laurie A. Van Egeren

The ethnic backgrounds and cultural variations of the people of Latin America are highly diverse. The term "Latin American" refers to individuals from Mexico, Central America, or South America with a Spanish surname or whose primary language is Spanish or Portuguese (Slonim, 1991), and is, strictly speaking, not applicable to all people living in these regions. However, for parsimony's sake, this chapter will refer to Mexican and Central and South American infants as Latin American.

The majority of inhabitants are at least partially descended from the native Indian population, which encompassed both more primitive hunter-gatherer societies and elaborate civilizations such as were developed by the Inca, Aztec, and Maya Indians. However, mixed heritage is the rule rather than the exception. European immigration has had a significant impact on the region; the Spaniards and Portuguese arrived in the sixteenth century, followed by large numbers of Germans and Italians in the late 1800s and early 1900s and Central Europeans after World War II. In addition, the importation of an estimated four million Africans (and perhaps two or three times that number) as slave workers changed the face of the population, particularly in Brazil. More recently, Asians, particularly the Japanese and Chinese, have made parts of South America their home. The original Indian societies were rich and varied, and each group of immigrants has incorporated their unique values and traditions. Clearly, no simple way exists to categorize the people of these countries.

To illustrate the extensive cultural variation of Latin America, a number of South American Indian groups reside in the Amazon Basin, maintaining virtual isolation from the industrialized world and practicing traditional rituals that might be interpreted as mutilation by outsiders; yet at the same time, most Latin American people live in urban areas, working in industrial contexts familiar to most European Americans. In Central America alone, different ethnic groups have concentrated in specific regions: Indians in Guatemala, non-Hispanic whites in Costa Rica, blacks and mulattos in Panama and the Caribbean coastal plains, and mestizos (of mixed white and Indian background) in El Salvador, Nicaragua, and throughout the other countries. And whereas most Latin Americans' primary language is Spanish or Portuguese, English is preferred in Guyana, Dutch is spoken in Suriname, and in some native enclaves Indian dialects continue to endure.

Surprisingly, given the relative proximity of Latin America to the United States and the large influx of immigrants originating from these countries, virtually no published research on infancy is available; this chapter describes just 12 articles, most of which were published only recently. The majority (seven) were conducted in Mexico, with three in Central America (Guatemala and Costa Rica), and two in South America (Peru and Brazil). An examination of these studies reveals that for the most part, the influence of the multiple Latin American cultures upon infant development remains untapped. Instead, researchers have thus far chosen to focus on basic survival issues, such as factors related to infant mortality and health. In a related vein, most of the studies have been conducted with the poorest, most disadvantaged groups, particularly Indians in rural areas.

Concentration on these issues is understandable. Much of Latin America has severe problems with overpopulation resulting from high birthrates and decreasing death rates. Furthermore, although most Latin American countries have focused on increasing the educational and economic opportunities of their people, these attempts have been only partially successful. The economies of most Latin American countries are in the process of development as the rural farm population migrates to urban centers in the face of increasing industrialization. In addition, high rates of inflation, massive foreign debt, and smoldering political tensions have plagued many regions, contributing to poverty, inadequate health care, and illiteracy.

Within this context, the minimal literature on Latin American infants is primarily descriptive, identifying patterns of behavior and a number of factors that appear to place infants at risk for poor health or early death. In keeping with findings from other developing nations in Asia and Africa, as well from minority groups in the United States, younger mothers are more likely to have babies prone to serious health problems (Palloni, Aguirre & Lastiri, 1994, 268). Frequent childbearing also takes a toll; when children are born more closely spaced and a greater number of children are born to a mother, subsequent infants are placed at greater risk for death (Haines & Avery, 1982, 264; Palloni, Aguirre & Lastiri, 1994, 268; Schieber et al., 1994, 271). These risk factors are interrelated. Higher fertility rates are more prevalent among rural, less educated women, who often live in less sanitary conditions, may have difficulty obtaining access to adequate health care, and are more likely to use traditional birth attendants (Haines & Avery, 1982, 264; Scheiber et al., 1994, 271). One measure to prevent poor infant outcomes is breastfeeding (Palloni, Aguirre & Lastiri, 1994, 268), and a few studies have examined the role of feeding practices in the survival of Latin American infants. Perez-Escamilla, and Dewey (1992, 269) determined that Mexico has particularly low rates of breast-feeding; in fact, by six months of age, only 10% continue to be breast-fed (Leyva-Pacheco, Bacardi-Gascon & Jimenez-Cruz, 1994, 265).

Interestingly, only one study on infant health and mortality has explored the unique cultural practices that contribute to and maintain health-related behaviors. Escobar, Salazar, and Chuy (1983, 263) discuss beliefs about the etiology of diarrhea, which can be fatal to young children, held by a sample of low-SES Peruvian women. These beliefs include treatment by withholding milk from the infants, which the authors suggest may be related to declining breast-feeding rates. Much more research is needed to investigate the role that cultural traditions play in maternal health attributions and treatment choices.

A few studies have examined more general issues related to infant psychosocial development. For example, Brazelton (1972, 262) found that among the Mayan Indians, where quiet, compliant child behavior is valued, the specific constellation of child-rearing practices does indeed produce calm, nonexploratory infants. Another researcher investigated whether previous findings of advanced motor development in less-developed countries (studied primarily in Africa) held true in Brazil as well; it did not, suggesting that less economic development is not a marker of precocious motor behavior (Paine, 1983, 267). Rather, in contrast to Africa, where early crawling and walking has an adaptive function and mothers assist their children in developing motor skills, Brazilian cultural mores do not place a premium on early motor development. In a rare examination of the role of the father in the family, Regalski and Gaulin (1993, 270) studied perceptions of whom infants are considered to physically resemble on paternal confidence in a sample of Mexicans from the Yucatan. Language development also has been explored among Guatemalan Indians (Wilhite, 1983, 273). In the only study in this chapter to compare infant development in two cultures, sleeping arrangements of Mayan and United States infants showed markedly different patterns; whereas all Mayan infants slept with their mothers, no infants from the U.S. did (Morelli et al., 1992, 266). This research clearly highlights the priority on interdependence in Latin America as compared to the focus on independence in the white Americans.

Given the extreme paucity of research conducted to date with Latin American infants and families, the field is wide open for investigation. Survival needs must continue to be addressed: birth-weight and perinatal survival, infant and child mortality, and physical growth and nutritional needs. However, in addition to describing rates of mortality and patterns of growth, cultural attitudes, beliefs, values, and traditions that maintain risk factors or contribute to resilience must also be investigated. Furthermore, beyond the few studies described in this chapter, research is notably absent on the social environment of Latin American infants, especially given the strong emphasis these cultures place on kinship bonds, extended family relationships, respect for elder family members, and a collective worldview. Current research conducted in more industrialized countries points to the differential role of culture in infant psychophysiological development. Yet it appears that investigators are of the mind that before we study such issues in Mexico, Central America, and South America, basic needs must first be addressed. Interestingly, however, similar economic and political difficulties are present in many African nations, yet the African infancy literature contains studies examining not only mortality and birth-weight, but also child-rearing practices and other psychosocial questions. Perhaps an additional area of investigation would query reasons that so little research is conducted in Latin America compared to other regions; only then can we begin to remedy this glaring omission in our knowledge of the world's children.

REFERENCES

Greenfield, P.M. (1994). Independence and interdependence as developmental scripts: Implications for theory, research, and practice. In P.M. Greenfield & R.R. Cocking, *Cross-cultural roots of child development* (pp. 1–35). Hillsdale, NJ: Erlbaum.

Slonim, M.B. (1991). *Children, culture, and ethnicity: Evaluating and understanding the impact.* New York: Garland.

RESOURCES

262. Brazelton, T.B. (1972). Implications of infant development among the Mayan Indians of Mexico. *Human Development, 15,* 90–111.

  Mayan descendants bear quiet, alert infants fitted to the quieting child-rearing practices to which they are exposed in their mothers' *rebozos*. The belly cinch, the *rebozo*, covered faces, and frequent breast-feedings to quiet the infant produce imitative, nonexploratory infants who develop in a slightly delayed (about one month) but parallel fashion to U.S. infants in motor, mental, and social parameters.

263. Escobar, G., Salazar, E., & Chuy, M. (1983). Beliefs regarding the etiology and treatment of infantile diarrhea in Lima, Peru. *Social Science and Medicine, 17,* 1257–1269.

  Interviews were conducted with low-SES women (91 mothers of children under age 2, 25 other mothers, and 23 secondary students) in Lima, Peru. Results indicate that diarrhea is not seen as an infectious disease, but is placed in the framework of the hot-cold dichotomy prevalent in Latin America; that is, diarrhea is believed to be caused by invasion of the body by cold or by ingestion of foods designated as "cold." Suspension of milk consumption is thought to be an essential part of treatment, a significant finding in view of the decline in breast-feeding.

264. Haines, M., & Avery, R. (1982). Differential infant and child mortality in Costa Rica: 1968–1973. *Population Studies, 36,* 31–43.

Data from the 1973 census was used to analyze the correlates of differences in infant and child mortality in Costa Rica for 1968–1973. Provision of Peru medical services and education of women related to lower child mortality. Sanitation and SES have a weaker but important effect. Fertility and mortality appear to have a significant causal interaction.

265. Leyva Pacheco, R., Bacardi-Gascon, M., & Jimenez-Cruz, A. (1994). Variables associated with breast-feeding patterns in Tijuana, Mexico. *Salud Publica de Mexico, 36,* 161–167.

This study examined the prevalence of feeding patterns among infants born in Tijuana, Mexico. The most usual feeding patterns were: at three months of age, breast milk plus formula; at six months, formula plus other foods; and at 12 months, fresh milk plus other foods. Three infants were never breast-fed; at three months, 43% of the infants were not receiving their mother's milk; and at six months, 90% were dependent on formula and other food only.

266. Morelli, G., Oppenheim, D., Rogoff, B., & Goldsmith, D. (1992). Cultural variation in infants' sleeping arrangements: Questions of independence. *Developmental Psychology, 28,* 604–613.

The parents of 14 Mayan infants and 18 U.S. infants were questioned on the sleep arrangements for the infants and the parents. None of the U.S. infants regularly slept with their mothers during their first two years, whereas all of the Mayan infants slept with their mothers. The U.S. mothers cited reasons of wanting to foster independence with the infants and the Mayan mothers were trying to foster closeness.

267. Paine, P.A. (1983). Is motor development really more advanced in third world infants? *Perceptual & Motor Skills, 57,* 729–730.

Motor and adaptive development at 4, 8, 12, and 18 months in Brazilian infants of mixed racial descent were studied. Gesell Developmental Schedule quotients were similar to those found in American black and white infants; thus, the phenomenon of precocious motor development was not confirmed in the Brazilian infants.

268. Palloni, A., Aguirre, G., & Lastiri, S. (1994). The effects of breast-feeding and the pace of childbearing on early childhood mortality in Mexico. *Bulletin of the Pan-American Health Organization, 28,* 93–111.

Data from Mexico's Demographic and Health Survey (1987) on 2,665 children born between 1982 and 1986 indicate strong negative effects of breast-feeding on infant mortality, especially among infants under 6 months old. An integrated model suggests that the effects of improved birth spacing and maternal age at delivery can decrease infant morality by 20% to 40%, but the effects of reduced breast-feeding could offset these benefits by more than 60%.

269. Perez-Escamilla, R., & Dewey, K.G. (1992). The epidemiology of breast-feeding in Mexico: Rural vs. urban areas. *Bulletin of the Pan-American Health Organization, 26,* 30–36.

Data suggest that Mexican rates of initiation of breast-feeding are among the lowest found in developing countries. The median duration of breast-feeding in 1987 was virtually the same as it had been in 1976, and about half of all Mexican infants are not breast-fed beyond six months of age.

270. Regalski, J., & Gaulin, S. (1993). Whom are Mexican infants said to resemble? Monitoring and fostering paternal confidence in the Yucatan. *Ethology and Sociobiology, 14,* 97–113.

Interviews with the 198 parents and relatives of Mexican infants under age 6 months in Ticul, Yucatan, indicate that infants are said to resemble their fathers much more frequently than their mothers, especially for low-birth-order children and when the parents have been paired only briefly. The presence of the father has no effect on mothers' tendencies to allege paternal resemblance, and children named after the father are not more likely to be said to resemble him.

271. Schieber, B., O'Rourke, K., Rodriguez, C., & Bartlett, A. (1994). Risk factor analysis of peri-neonatal mortality in rural Guatemala. *Bulletin of the Pan-American Health Organization,, 28,* 229–238.

Mothers whose infants had died between week 20 of pregnancy and day 28 of life and mothers whose infants had survived at least 28 days after birth were interviewed (n=120) for both groups. Malpresentation, prolonged labor, preterm labor, second pregnancy in 12 months, and greater number of pregnancies were significant predictors of mortality. Increased risk was also associated with birth delivery by a traditional birth attendant; however, women using such attendants were more likely to be illiterate and of lower SES than women using physicians.

272. Vazquez, M., Pearson, P.B., & Beauchamp, G.K. (1982). Flavor preferences in malnourished Mexican infants. *Physiology Behavior, 28,* 513–519.

Taste and flavor preferences were evaluated in malnourished (n = 113) and well-nourished Mexican infants tested between 2 and 24 months of age. The preferences of malnourished children for NaCl, citric acid, and urea were not substantially different. In sucrose tests, malnourished infants exhibited a decreased response. Malnourished infants ingested more casein hydrolysate and soup solution than soup alone. All infants exhibited a preference for soup with MSG relative to plain soup.

273. Wilhite, M. (1983). Children's acquisition of language routines: The end-of-meal routine in Cakchiquel. *Language in Society, 12,* 47–64.

In acquiring language, children must acquire not only the structure of the language, but also the rules for using language appropriately in a wide variety of situations. This field study reports the acquisition by 143 one- to ten-year-old children of a routine used at the end of meals by Cakchiquel-speaking Indians in Guatemala. Examination of data on the use of the end-of-meal routines revealed the order of acquisition of the elements of the routine.

PART 3
EUROPE

7 THE CULTURAL DIVERSITY OF INFANTS RESIDING IN EUROPEAN COUNTRIES

AN EXAMINATION OF THE LITERATURE

Domini R. Castellino

Dating as far back as prehistoric time, Europe has been and continues to be occupied by numerous peoples and nations. Although the second-smallest continent in the world, Europe boosts the second- largest population of all the continents. Europe contains a number of peninsulas such as the Iberian, Italian, and Kola, as well as a large number of offshore islands, including Sicily, Crete, and the British Isles. Moreover, the various countries contained within Europe, such as Germany, France, Ireland, and the Scandinavian countries, generate a variety of cultures and ethnic groups.

Although many nations are, in general, comprised of one dominant cultural group, immigration is slowly diversifying many European countries. For example, a large proportion of Asian Turks, Arabs, and black Africans reside in western Europe. Moreover, the breakup of the Union of Soviet Socialist Republics (USSR) led to the formation of 15 individual republics, each with its own dominant ethnic group. Thus, when referring to the cultural context of European infants, numerous and diverse cultural standards, values, histories, and norms must be considered.

Consequently, problems may arise for social scientists conducting research on these populations due to potential barriers such as language differences, cultural values, time, and money. In addition, designing "contextually sensitive" measures and deciding when it is appropriate to use similar constructs for groups of different race, ethnicity, and social class is an arduous task.

The current chapter describes only 19 studies that have been published on various groups of infants residing in several European countries and locations, the majority of which have been conducted in the 1980s and the 1990s. Much of the research reviewed here involves infants with diversified backgrounds, ranging from English, Vietnamese, North African, Asian, Bangladeshi, and West Indian, who are currently living in several European locations. Nevertheless, a close examination of the current literature provides information on a very limited number of topics related to infants. Specifically, several of the studies focused on physical growth and development (Child, 1983, 275; Collet et al., 1986, 276; Davies & Wheeler, 1989, 277; Doornbos et al., 1991, 278; Mason, Davies & Marshall, 1982, 285), some centered on infant feeding practices (Lithell, 1981, 283; Scott, 1975, 290), and many focused on issues pertaining to infant mortality, including three with a specific focus on the incidence of, and factors relating to, sudden infant death dyndrome (SIDS) (Faroogi, Perry & Beevers, 1993, 239; Faroogi, 1994, 280; Gantley, Davies & Murcott, 1993, 281). Only 2 of the 18 research investigations were related to any aspect of infant social development (Child, 1983, 275; Rabain-Jamin & Sabeau-Jouannet, 1997, 288). Specifically, one study investigated infant play behaviors, and the other focused on mother-infant attachment. None of the studies examined infant cognitive, perceptual, language, or emotional development.

Although research on infants of color in Europe is not substantial, the investigations that have been conducted and reviewed in the current chapter reveal several interesting findings. For example, a study by Sagi, Van Ijzendoorn, and Koren-Karie (1991, 289) on infant attachment examined the scores from the Strange Situation procedure of infants from several different countries including Holland, Germany, Sweden, Israel, and the United States. The investigators found that infants' behavior prior to the separation episode was indicative of the attachment classification that was ultimately given to the infant. They also reported that both within and across cultures, scores from the Strange Situation procedure differed considerably.

This study raised the question of the validity of this procedure for assessing infant attachments, particularly across cultures. It may be that the Strange Situation procedure is not sensitive to the many cultural differences that exist between infants and families with diverse ethnic and cultural backgrounds. For instance, on average approximately two-thirds of North American infants are classified as being securely attached (Fogel, 1991). In contrast, almost 50% of German infants are classified as avoidant using this same procedure (Grossman et al., 1985). This striking disparity in attachment classification may be attributable to differences in socialization and child-rearing practices across cultures. The behaviors indicative of an avoidant classification according to American standards may simply be representative of the behaviors and norms that are valued in the German culture. For instance, German children are raised to be respectful and obedient, in an atmosphere that fosters self-sufficiency and discourages public displays of emotion (Slonim, 1991). Consequently, these values that are encouraged and expected within the German culture may account for the kinds of behaviors observed in contexts such as the Strange Situation. This example not only raises the question of the validity of the Strange Situation procedure for assessing infant attachment across cultures, but also provides evidence for the importance of conducting research that is sensitive to various cultures and ethnicities.

Numerous other studies contained in the current chapter pertain to the physical development of infants, the preponderant majority of which are comparative in nature. For example, weights were compared in several of the studies among French-born North African (Collett et al., 1986, 276), British-born Asian (Mason, Davies & Marshall, 1982, 285), and Bangladeshi infants (Davies & Wheeler, 1989, 277). It appears that research focused on the overall physical well-being of infants in these cultures is of central concern. Sixteen of the 18 studies examined basic survival issues: namely, physical growth, feeding, and infant mortality. Furthermore, studies regarding the parental feeding practices of infants in Europe were consistent with the results found in other studies of this nature. For example, Vietnamese parents living in London preferred bottle-feeding over breast-feeding their infants (Sharma, 1994, 291), consistent with studies of Asian American infants living in the United States whose parents also preferred bottle-feeding to breast-feeding (ex., see Chapter 3 Fishman, 1988, 191; Serdula et al., 1991, 195).

Other investigations examined the incidence of sudden infant death syndrome in Asian and white infants living in the United Kingdom. Results indicated a lower death rate associated with SIDS for Asian infants as compared to white infants (Faroogi, 1994, 280; Faroogi, Perry & Beevers, 1993, 279). The authors suggest that these results may be due to the fact that more white infants are placed in the prone position for sleeping and, in addition, Asian infants are more likely to sleep in their parents' bedroom. Comparative studies such as these can provide valuable information to aid in the prevention of negative or even detrimental infant outcomes, such as SIDS.

Although by no means exhaustive, the research contained in the citations that follow provide some insight into the behavior and development of European infants with many diverse backgrounds. However, this is just a beginning. Much more research is needed on various social, emotional, and psychological topics, research that considers the diversity of cultures and contexts within which these infants and families are embedded, in order to gain a better understanding of the behavior and development of European infants and their families. Moreover, larger samples both within and across ethnic and cultural groups and more sophisticated methodology are also critical to the future of research in this field.

REFERENCES

Fogel, A. (1991). *Infancy: Infant, family, and society*. St. Paul, MN: West.

Grossman, K., Grossman, K.E., Spangler, G., Suess, G., & Unzner, L. (1985). Maternal sensitivity and newborns' orientation responses as related to quality of attachment in northern Germany. *Monographs of the Society for Research in Child Development, 50*(Serial No. 209), 233–256.

Slonim, M.B. (1991). *Children, culture, and ethnicity*. New York: Garland.

RESOURCES

274. Alvearm, J., & Brooke, O.G. (1978). Fetal growth in different racial groups. *Archives of the Diseases of Childhood, 53*, 27–32.

Northern European, black, and Indian Asian mothers and their newborns were matched for parity, gestational age, sex, maternal age, maternal smoking habits, and social class. Indian Asian infants, however, were lighter and had smaller head and limb circumferences than the other groups, although their linear measurements were the same. Black and European infants were almost identical in size. No effects on any of the fetal measurements were attributed to smoking.

275. Child, E. (1983). Play and culture: A study of English and Asian children. *Leisure Studies, 2*, 169–186.

The importance of sociocultural factors in preschoolers' play behaviors was examined in 61 English children from working- and middle-class backgrounds and 89 Sikh, Muslim, and Hindu children. The ages of the children ranged from 22 to 55 months. Results suggested that children's social group membership was associated with differences in the style and content of play. Class and cultural groups seemed to differentiate the preschoolers' motivations, behavior patterns, and social cues.

276. Collet, J.P., Lacroix-Liberas, S., Routhier, J.L., Piens, A., Mamelle, N., Hermier, M., & Francois, R. (1986). Growth from birth to 2 years of North African infants born in France. *Archives of French Pediatrics, 43*, 61–65.

Weights and heights from birth to age two were measured for North African infants born in France. These measurements were compared to standard growth curves for French infants and to the growth of French infants living in similar conditions. There were no differences in growth rates for height, but North African female infants were heavier at six to nine months of age.

277. Davies, A.G., & Wheeler, E. (1989). Analysis of the weights of infants of Bangladeshi origin attending two clinics in Tower Hamlets. *Child Care, Health and Development, 15*, 167–174.

Weight data was gathered on 220 Bangladeshi infants. The mean weights of the Bangledeshi infants at birth and 6 and 18 months of age were lower than the Tanner-Whitehouse fiftith percentiles (obtained from British children). The sample means were similar to those reported for well-nourished Indian infants, suggesting that these are a more appropriate reference group for Bangledeshi infants than the Tanner-Whitehouse values.

278. Doornbos, J.P., Nordbeck, H.J., Van-Enk, A.E., Muller, A.S., & Treffers, P.E. (1991). Differential birthweights and the clinical relevance of birthweight standards in a multiethnic society. *International Journal of Gynaecology and Obstetrics, 34*, 319–324.

BW and related variables were analyzed from a sample of over 25,000 infants born in Amsterdam. The BW difference between Dutch and Asian infants disappeared after allowing for maternal height. Mediterranean infants displayed higher means than other groups, whereas black infants showed lower means. The authors suggest that the current BW standards are inappropriate for determining deviant weight in non-Dutch samples.

279. Faroogi, S., Perry, I.J., & Beevers, D.G. (1993). Ethnic differences in infant-rearing practices and their possible relationship to the incidence of sudden infant death syndrome (SIDS). *Paediatric Perinatal Epidemiology, 7,* 245–252.

In the United Kingdom, the incidence of SIDS is considerably lower in infants of Asian origin. A study of 202 white and 172 Asian multiparous mothers found that significantly more white infants (31%) than Asians (11%) were placed in the prone position at night and that 94% of Asian infants slept in their parents' bedroom, compared with 61% of whites. These findings suggest that the prone position and separate bedrooms may be contributors to the development of SIDS.

280. Faroogi, S. (1994). Ethnic differences in infant care practices and in the incidence of sudden infant death syndrome in Birmingham. Conference on Ethnicity and the Sudden Infant Death Syndrome (1993, Cardiff, Wales). *Early Human Development, 38,* 209–213.

A survey of 202 white and 172 Asian women in the United Kingdom during the first year of their youngest child's life indicated that almost three times as many white infants were placed in a prone sleeping position, which is associated with an increased risk of SIDS. Almost all of the Asian infants slept in the same bed or the same room as their parents, whereas one-third of the white infants slept alone. These Asian infant care practices may provide more protection against the risk of SIDS.

281. Gantley, M., Davies, D.P., & Murcott, A. (1993). Sudden infant death syndrome: Links with infant care practices. *British Medical Journal, 306,* 16–20.

British women of Bangladeshi or Welsh origin with infants under one year of age were interviewed to examine practices that contribute to the low incidence of SIDS in Asian populations. Infants of Welsh origin were more likely to undergo various periods of high and low sensory input. Alternatively, the infants of Bangladeshi origin were surrounded by a consistently rich sensory environment. The results suggest that long periods of solitary, quiet sleep may be a contributing factor to the higher incidence of SIDS in white infants as compared to Asian infants.

282. Hopkins, B. (1976). Culturally determined patterns of handling the human infant. *Journal of Human Movement Studies, 2,* 1–27.

The infant handling patterns of 48 West Indian mothers residing in Britain were studied. A West Indian formal handling routine is described in detail. Findings indicated that the extent of the formal handling routine used with the infant was related to behavioral characteristics that the newborn exhibited before the routine was initiated.

283. Lithell, U. (1981). Breast-feeding habits and their relation to infant mortality and marital fertility. *Journal of Family History, 6,* 182–194.

An investigation was conducted of the impact of breast-feeding habits on age-specific marital fertility from 1826 to 1870 in two Swedish-speaking communities. In Petalax, fertility and mortality rates were high, whereas in Rodon they were low. In Petalax, cessation of lactation led to increased fertility and shorter intervals between pregnancies. In Rodon, prolonged nursing helped to protect infants against disease and increased the interval between pregnancies.

284. Lyon, A.J., Clarkson, P., Jeffrey, I., & West, G.A. (1994). Effect of ethnic origin of mother on fetal outcome. *Archives of Disease in Childhood: Fetal and Neonatal Edition, 70,* 40–43.

Asian, African, and West Indian infants born in London were studied from weeks gestational age to determine fetal outcomes. Asian and white infants had similar perinatal death rates. Significantly more intrauterine deaths and neonatal deaths occurred for infants with mothers from Africa and the West Indies than for those with white mothers. It is unclear why black women were more likely to experience preterm labor; one contributing factor may be differences in intrauterine infection rates.

285. Mason, E.S., Davies, D.P., & Marshall, W.A. (1982). Early postnatal weight gain: Comparisons between Asian and Caucasian infants. *Early Human Development, 6,* 253–255.

Examination of early weight gain patterns of British-born Asian and Caucasian infants indicated that the Asian infants were lighter at birth. The rate of their weight gain was not significantly different from the Caucasian infants. These results offer indirect support for the idea that the smaller size at birth found in Asian infants is not due to intrauterine growth retardation.

286. Mavlanov, K.U., Grafova, V.A., & Orlova, S.V. (1992). Seasonal dynamics of the indices of humoral immunity in children aged 3 months to 1 year in relation to nutrition in an arid zone. *Voprosy-Pitaniia, 4,* 26–29.

Seasonal data on humoral immunity of 245 Turkmen and 240 European infants aged 3 to 12 months indicate that in summer there were reduced levels of IgM, IgG in the serum, and insufficient supply with thiamine and ascorbic acid. IgA serum level was the lowest in spring. Changes in humoral immunity in summer are associated with an increase of intestinal diseases and lower body mass. (In Russian)

287. Pickering, R., Murray, G., & Forbes, J. (1986). Pre-term fetal life times in Scotland. *Population Studies, 40,* 115–127.

A proportional hazards model was used to evaluate the association between 10 categorical covariates and the risk of preterm delivery for women having their first child and women experiencing subsequent pregnancies. For both groups of women, age and a history of abortion were major factors associated with increased hazard. A history of perinatal death was also associated with substantially increased hazard to the pregnancy for multiparous women.

288. Rabain-Jamin, J., & Sabeau-Jouannet, E. (1997). Maternal speech to 4-month-old infants in two cultures: Wolof and French. *International Journal of Behavioral Development, 20(3),* 425–451.

This study examines the infant-directed speech of the two cultures in order the see how the infant-directed communicative acts relate to the value system of the cultures. The results suggest that cultural factors influence the communicative acts. It was also found that both cultures use a high percentage of expressive speech.

289. Sagi, A., Van Ijzendoorn, M., & Koren-Karie, N. (1991). Primary appraisal of the Strange Situation: A cross-cultural analysis of preseparation episodes. *Developmental Psychology, 27,* 587–596.

Seven laboratories in different countries (among them, Germany, Holland, Israel, Japan, Sweden, and the United States; *n* = 498) conducted the Strange Situation to try to determine if the infant's behavior prior to the separation experience was indicative of the separation classification ultimately given. They found that, indeed, the preseparation experience was indicative of the attachment classification given based on the reunion episode. In addition, the Strange Situation scores were markedly different across and within cultures, raising the question of validity of attachment scores across cultures.

290. Scott, S. (1975). White and West Indian infants in London: Development from birth to 44 weeks of age. *Child-Care, Health & Development, 1,* 203–215.

Fifty white and 50 West Indian infants were examined on four occasions between birth and 10 months of age. The West Indian babies were significantly advanced at birth, but by 6 weeks were losing their advantage, and had no significant differences at 6 and 10 months of age. Factors considered were the ethnic origin, growth patterns, feeding customs, and relevant socioeconomic factors.

291. Sharma, A. (1994). The availability of advice regarding infant feeding to immigrants of Vietnamese origin: A survey of families and health visitors. *Child Care, Health & Development, 20,* 349–354.

This study of 40 Vietnamese women in London indicated that traditional Vietnamese feeding methods, especially breast-feeding, are being abandoned. The majority of women in Vietnam breast-fed their infants, but since arriving in Britain, most Vietnamese mothers switched to bottle-feeding.

292. Singer, B., & Wolfsdorf, J. (1975). Early discharge of infants of low birth weight: A prospective study. *British Medical Journal, 1,* 362–364.

Outcomes were studied for a group of LBW African infants. Readmission rates were much higher for LBW infants, with the bronchopneumonia associated with hypothermia recorded as the most common reason for readmission. Morbidity and mortality were significantly related to the incidence of hypothermia. The mortality rate of twins was three times greater than singletons in the same group.

293. Trapp, P., Mielke, J., Jorde, L., & Eriksson, A. (1983). Infant mortality patterns in Aland, Finland. *Human Biology, 55,* 131–149.

Infant mortality in Aland, Finland, from 1751 to 1935 was examined. A steady decline in mortality rates and a reduction in year-to-year variation began in about 1810 and was linked to medical innovations, decreases in household and family size, and socioeconomic changes. Regional variation in infant mortality rates do not appear to be shaped by either geographic location of parishes or population density. A time-series analysis demonstrates that high birthrates tend to co-occur with periods of high infant mortality.

PART 4
AFRICA

8 INFANCY RESEARCH IN AFRICA

AN ABUNDANCE OF RICH RESEARCH OPPORTUNITIES

Rosalind B. Johnson

The continent of Africa is divided into more than 50 nations and fragmented into at least twice as many ethnic and linguistic groups. Though the term "African" is widely used throughout the world to describe inhabitants of Africa, this term does not capture the ethnic and cultural diversity of the continent. The population of African nations is mostly made up of indigenous persons, however, several prominent groups emigrated from European countries and India. This combination of people has created an abundance of variation in the traditions and values of Africa.

An examination of the various ethnic and linguistic groups provides an understanding and appreciation of the rich cultural heritage of Africa. Traditionally, African cultures are thought to be based on kinship groups and a sense of oneness with nature. These traditions and values are demonstrated through the philosophy that underlies child-rearing in Africa (Slonim, 1991). Children are highly valued in African families. For example, in many African cultures a formal ceremony marks the first time a child is brought outside of the home (Slonim, 1991). Once outside there is a sense of shared responsibility for child-rearing that is demonstrated in the African proverb, "It takes a village to raise a child."

Grandparents, especially grandmothers, have a special role in raising the children in the community. Grandparents are seen as the link with familial histories, other traditions, and values (Slonim, 1991). In general, the continent of Africa possesses an enormous amount of rich research opportunities regarding children and families.

Even though a large percentage of Africa's population is under the age of six and Africa as a whole contains more than 10% of the world's population, there is limited published research on African infants. The limited research is especially surprising since there is anthropological research to support the notion that infants and children are central to African cultures (Slonim, 1991).

This chapter reviews 41 articles, published between 1970 and 1996. About 29% of the articles were published in the 1970s. Eleven of the studies were conducted in South Africa, and 19 involve samples from West and Central Africa. Five studies included samples from North and East Africa. Extremely few studies have been reported from countries in the northern part of Africa.

Twelve countries (Algeria, Egypt, Ghana, Kenya, Malawi, Mali, Nigeria, Senegal, Sierra Leone, Uganda, Zaire, and Zambia) of 50 nations were found to have published research about their infants. This means that only 26% of African countries are represented in the infancy literature being reviewed in this chapter.

Many African nations share a mission of alleviating economic, educational, health, and political difficulties faced by people. These problems have had a profound impact on African infants. Most of the African infancy research focuses on risk factors related to infant mortality and morbidity, and basic variables such as feeding and parenting (Aly, 1990, 294; deVries, 1984, 301; Dorjahn, 1976, 303; Ebomoyi, Adetoro & Wickremasinghe, 1991, 304; Harrison et al., 1993, 307; Isaac & Feinberg, 1982, 310; Muhudhia & Musoke, 1989, 321; Richter, 1989, 326; Retel-Lauretin & Benoit, 1976, 328; Tabutin, 1974, 333).

Due to the high incidence of malnutrition and starvation among infants in African countries, research has focused on breast-feeding and weaning. For example, Dettwyler (1986, 299; 1987, 300) found that Malinese West African mothers breast-fed on demand and weaned before age two. Dettwyler suggests that early weaning contributes to the high incidence of malnutrition during infancy.

This literature also focuses on descriptions of socioeconomic factors, which make infant development challenging in African countries. These socioeconomic factors include maternal education (Ivanans, 1975, 311), household density (Richter, 1989, 326), and marital status (Kilbride & Kilbride, 1974, 313). For instance, Konczacki (1972, 315) found that for sub-Saharan African families, maternal socioeconomic variables contributed to severe infant malnutrition. In general, mothers of premature and LBW infants were poorly educated, and had low incomes and unplanned pregnancies. It seems to be universal that the status of the mother is a good indicator of infant development.

Six studies addressed issues other than those associated with risk. These studies examined cognitive development (Richter & Grieve, 1991, 327), cradling preferences (Saling, Abrams & Chesler, 1983, 330; Saling, 1984, 331), mother-infant interaction (Goldberg, 1972, 306; Lusk & Lewis,

1972, *320;* Tronick, Morelli & Ivey, 1992, *334*), motor development (Cintas, 1989, *297*), personality (Super, Harkness & LeVine, 1974, *331*), temperament (DeVries, 1984, *301;* Super, 1976, *332*) and visual habituation of African infants (Lecuyer & Tano, 1990, *318*). For example, deVries and Sameroff (1984, *302*) examined the influence of the environment on infant temperament among East African infants from three societies. Lecuyer and Tano (1990, *318*) explored differences in visual habituation rate among French and Ivory Coast infants. Most of these were cross-cultural comparative studies.

There were several studies that looked at fetal movements and their relationship to neonatal competency (Irwin-Carruthers, 1995, *309*) and sleeping positions of infants in South Africa (Potgieter & Kibel, 1992, *325*). There is also one study that examined cross-cultural differences among parents who were given information that their child was physically and/or mentally disabled (Krauss-Mars, 1994, *316*). In addition, there was one study of child abuse in Nigeria (Okeahialam, 1984, *323*). Child abuse has received little attention in research in Africa, but with the increase in the abandonment of infants and child labor and exploitation, there has been an increase in the interest of child abuse.

LIMITATIONS OF CURRENT LITERATURE

Markedly missing are studies on father-infant interactions, transition to parenthood, and language development. The lack of studies on language development is especially surprising given rich diversity of African languages. In addition, research in urban, developed areas of Africa is limited. There is no clear explanation for the limited interest in these areas. Certainly, economic, political, and religious factors influence the societal agenda with respect to investing in studies of human development.

Another reason for the lack of research in Africa is suggested by the comparative approach taken by researchers; an approach that stimulates cross-race comparisons at the expense of within-race variation (Burlew et al., 1992). A reliance on a European American cultural framework for research may explain the reluctance of African countries to expose their children to Western researchers (Burlew et al., 1992). There is also the possibility that researchers have little interest or incentives to study infant development in Africa.

Nevertheless, African infancy literature consists of more than birthweight, morbidity, and mortality topics when compared to developing nations in Central and South America, it still falls short of reflecting the rich, diverse research opportunities available to be studied. Economic and political difficulties are responsible for some of the shortcomings in African infancy literature; however, one cannot discount stereotypes toward African people.

FUTURE DIRECTIONS IN RESEARCH

Based on this review, minimal African infancy literature is available to researchers. There is no doubt that valuable knowledge regarding infant development can be learned from the exploration of African infant development. As economic and political tensions are alleviated in African nations, maybe researchers will take advantage of the vast uncharted infancy research opportunities available in African countries.

Collaborations between psychologists, anthropologists, and physicians may increase the research on infancy development. It is clear that many at-risk variables must be addressed in many parts of African; however, if researchers approach African countries with an acknowledgment of these issues and ways to help, opportunities may become more available.

REFERENCES

Burlew, A.K.H., Banks, W.C., McAdoo, H.P., & Azibo, D.A. (Eds.). (1992). *African American psychology: Theory, research and practice* (pp. 1–3). Newbury Park, CA: Sage.

Slonim, M.B. (1991). *Children, culture, and ethnicity: Evaluating and understanding the impact* (pp. 195–207). New York: Garland.

RESOURCES

294. Aly, H. (1990). Demographic and socioeconomic factors affecting infant mortality in Egypt. *Journal of Biosocial Science, 22,* 447–451.

Analyses of data from the 1980 World Fertility Survey for Egypt indicate that demographic factors had more effect than socioeconomic factors on infant mortality. No significant overall difference between rural and urban households was found; however, availability of an adequate sewage system was a significant contributor in rural areas, while water quality and room density were significant contributors in urban areas.

295. Bolton, K.D., Chalmers, B., Cooper, P.A., & Wainer, E.S. (1993). Black mothers' experiences of a neonatal care unit. *Journal of Reproductive and Infant Psychology, 11,* 229–234.

The demographic characteristics and self-reported needs of 201 black South African mothers of premature infants indicated that mothers were poorly educated and had low incomes, and that their babies tended to be unplanned and had LBWs. Little preparation was provided prior to the mothers' contact with the NICU, and mothers were not given immediate access to their infants.

296. Borgerhoff-Mulder, M., & Milton, M. (1985). Factors affecting infant care in the Kipsigis. *Journal of Anthropological Research, 41,* 231–262.

Examination of variations in the quality of infant care and the symptoms of infant distress in Kipsigis infants indicated that the mother's absence does not affect either. Caretakers provide infant care of quality equal to that provided by the mother, and they play a greater role in maintaining proximity with the infant. The quality of infant care does not differ between polygynous and monogamous households. Contrary to predictions, neither the number of coresident caretakers nor the observed number of caretakers had significant effects on the quality of infant care.

297. Cintas, H. (1989). Cross-cultural variation in infant motor development. *Physical and Occupational Therapy in Pediatrics, 8,* 1–20.

Infant development varies cross-culturally, indicating that scales may not be used across all cultures for use as a tool for explaining abnormal development. Motor development variation is considered along with differences in care practices, environmental stresses, and other selective factors in motor development. The study considers North American white and black, African, Asian, and American Indian infants.

298. Chalmers, B. (1996) Cross-cultural comparisons of birthing: Psycho-social issues in Western and African birth. *Psychology & Health, 12(1),* 11–21.

This study examines a variety of birth customs in terms of preparation for birth and parenthood, the place of delivery, psychosocial support at birth, pain management in labor, mother-infant contact after birth, and breast-feeding. This article also examines the impact of the transition taking place from the rural to the Urban in Africa.

299. Dettwyler, K.A. (1986). Infant feeding in Mali, West Africa: Variations in belief and practice. *Social Science and Medicine, 23,* 651–664.

Among peri-Ur residents of Mali, West Africa, infant growth patterns are associated with differences in maternal attitudes toward infant feeding practices. Three attitudes toward infant feeding were derived: (1) eight months of age is the appropriate point for children to begin solid food; (2) children should not be forced to eat if not hungry; and (3) only children know when they are hungry.

300. Dettwyler, K.A. (1987). Breastfeeding and weaning in Mali: Cultural context and hard data. *Social Science and Medicine, 24,* 633–644.

Breast-feeding and weaning patterns among Malinese West African females were examined over a two-year period. Nearly all the women breast-fed, and infants were nursed on demand. Infants were weaned at a mean age of 20.8 months. Breast-feeding and weaning practices were associated with the growth and development of infants over the study period.

301. deVries, M.W. (1984). Temperament and infant mortality among the Masai of East Africa. *American Journal of Psychiatry, 141,* 1189–1194.

It was hypothesized that Masai infants assessed as having difficult temperaments would be at greater risk for infant mortality in the harsh environment. Ten infants with difficult temperaments and 10 with easy temperaments were followed. The hypothesis was not supported; infants with difficult temperaments had a greater survival rate (only one death occurred in the difficult-temperament group, whereas five of seven infants with easy temperaments died).

302. deVries, M.W., & Sameroff, A.J. (1984). Culture and temperament: Influences on infant temperament in three East African societies. *American Journal of Orthopsychiatry, 54,* 83–96.

The influence of environment on infant temperament was investigated in East African infants from three societies, Kikuyu, Digo, and Masai. Data was collected through ethnographic observations of daily life, psychometric tests, and questionnaire-interviews about child rearing and social life. Results suggest that environmental factors, including cultural child rearing patterns, degree of modernization, maternal orientation, ecological setting, and specific early life events, predicted infant temperament characteristics.

303. Dorjahn, V.R. (1976). Rural-urban differences in infant and child mortality among the Temne of Kolifa. *Journal of Anthropological Research, 32,* 74–103.

Infant and child mortality rates were compared for the Temne residing in the rural chiefdom of Kolifa Mayoso and in the nearby provincial town of Magburaka in central Sierra Leone. Consistent with other data from West Africa, child mortality was relatively high for both rural and urban groups, although the mortality rate was lower in the urban population. The high early mortality rates were probably related to weaning.

304. Ebomoyi, E., Adetoro, O., & Wickremasinghe, A. (1991). Birthweight and sociobiological factors in Ilorin, Nigeria. *Journal of Biosocial Science, 23,* 417–423.

An investigation of social and biological factors influencing BW among 3,053 babies showed that maternal weight, height, age, education, ethnicity, and child's sex significantly affected infant BW.

305. Fagard, J., Jacquet, A.Y. (1996). Changes in reaching and grasping objects of different sizes between 7 and 13 months. *British Journal of Developmental Psychology, 14(1),* 65–78.

The onset of the use of two hands to grasp large objects was examined. The results suggest that infants do not show more bimanual reaching with large objects before 11 months of age.

306. Goldberg, S. (1972). Infant care and growth in urban Zambia. *Human Development, 15,* 77–89.

Mother-infant relationships were studied for 38 dyads in a Zambian suburb. The author makes the point that only in the U.S. do children sleep in separate quarters rather than having them in continuous contact like other cultures.

307. Harrison, G., Zaghloul, S., Galal, O., & Gabr, A. (1993). Breastfeeding and weaning in a poor urban neighborhood in Cairo, Egypt: Maternal beliefs and perceptions. *Social Science and Medicine, 36,* 1063–1069.

Despite evidence that early weaning in less-developed countries can lead to malnutrition and increased child mortality, the tradition of prolonged breast-feeding is reversing in Egypt. Various factors that diminish the quantity and quality of mother's milk are noted: for example, the infant's characteristics, the mother's psychological and physical state and diet, and culturally based beliefs such as fasting during the religious period of Ramadan.

308. Heymann, M. (1993). Early postnatal assessment of the newborn in the developing country: Malawi. *Assoication of Black Nursing Faculty in Higher Education Journal, 4,* 90–94.

Infant mortality is defined as the number of deaths in the first year of life for every 1,000 babies born alive. The author presents information on ways that relevant health care policies and the use of newborn assessment tools (e.g., the Newborn History and Physical Examination Form) can decrease the rate of infant deaths, specifically in Malawi, Central Africa.

309. Irwin-Carruthers, S.H. (1995). Fetal movements in mid-pregnancy and their relationship to neonatal competency. *South African Journal of Physiotherapy, 51,* 21–25.

This pilot study examined fetal movement patterns and neonatal competencies of black and white infants. In the neonatal period, sequential and isolated movements were predominant, and the proportion of sequential and isolated movements was correlated with the total number of fetal movements. More active fetal movement was also related to greater neonatal competency. More mature patterns of fetal movement were exhibited by black infants, who also demonstrated more optimal postural tone, greater motor maturity, and good orientation/alertness.

310. Isaac, B., & Feinberg, W. (1982). Marital form and infant survival among the Mende of rural upper Bambara Chiefdom, Sierra Leone. *Human Biology, 54,* 627–634.

This study explored the possible relationship between marital form (monogamy vs. polygyny) and reproductive success (as measured by survival to 18 months) in 9 villages of Upper Bambara Chiefdom, Sierra Leone. Although the independent variables were themselves strongly related, survival of children to 18 months was statistically independent of the age and marital situation of their mothers.

311. Ivanans, T. (1975). Effect of maternal education and ethnic background on infant development. *Archives of Disease in Childhood, 50,* 454–457.

The association between two variables, maternal education and ethnic background, and infant development was investigated in a sample of infants aged 3, 6, 9, and 12 months. Across all ethnic groups, infants of mothers with higher levels of education exhibited more advanced development than infants of mothers with lower levels of education. Among babies whose mothers had middle levels of education, North African infants were assessed at higher levels of development than European infants.

312. Kilbride, J.E., Robbins, M.C., & Kilbride, P.L. (1970). The comparative motor development of Baganda, American white, and American black infants. *American Anthropologist, 72,* 1422–1428.

This study examined the developmental motor quotients of 1- to 24-month-old infants. Infants were found to have significantly more advanced motor development in the first year of life when compared to the sample of white and black American children studied by N. Bayley.

313. Kilbride, P., & Kilbride, J. (1974). Sociocultural factors and the early manifestation of sociability behavior among Baganda infants. *Ethos, 2,* 296–314.

An attempt is made to investigate why Uganda's Baganda infants seem to be more advanced in psychomotor behavior. The mother's placidity and greater physical activity during pregnancy and her favorable acceptance of motherhood may be contributing factors. Data on infant sociability were gathered from parents in living in Kampala. Children are directly taught accepted social behavior at an early age. The social dynamic of status mobility was reflected in many adult values, which, through the socialization process, result in a measurable manifestation of sociability in early infancy.

314. Kilbride, P., & Kilbride, J. (1983). Socialization for high positive affect between mother and infant among the Baganda of Uganda. *Ethos, 11,* 232–245.

Differential emotions theory is supported by observational data of mother-child interaction during the first 8 months of life collected in 12 households of the Baganda society of Uganda. Baganda women display high positive affect toward their infants, though this is typically expressed only in private.

315. Konczacki, Z.A. (1972). Infant malnutrition in sub-Saharan Africa: A problem in socio-economic development. *Canadian Journal of African Studies, 6,* 433–449.

Substantial numbers of children aged six and under in sub-Saharan Africa are affected by some degree of protein-calorie malnutrition. Factors contributing to the severe malnutrition rates include cultural, ecological, and economic factors. Widespread infant malnutrition has very serious socioeconomic consequences and contributes to a general lack of motivation for individual achievement.

316. Krauss-Mars, A.H. (1994). Breaking bad news to parents with disabled children: A cross-cultural study. *Childcare, Health & Development, 20*, 101–113.

Experiences of mixed-race, black and white South African parents after being given the information that their child was physically and/or mentally disabled were investigated. Few black parents stated that their understanding of the diagnosis was verified. In contrast, white parents reported that the diagnosis was explained, but were more likely to deny the diagnosis of mental handicap than black or mixed-race parents. In general, parents felt satisfied with the way they were given the diagnosis.

317. Lasich, A.J. (1992). A study of referrals of black children to a general hospital psychiatric outpatient clinic. *Australian & New Zealand Journal of Psychiatry, 26*, 467–473.

Retrospective demographic and clinical data for African and Indian South African child psychiatric outpatients were examined. The most common reasons for referral were poor school performance and behavioral problems, and the most common diagnoses were mental retardation and epilepsy. Referrals were influenced by socioeconomic and political factors, a scarcity of school psychological services, and limited facilities for developmentally delayed children.

318. Lecuyer, R., & Tano, J. (1990). Speed of visual habituation among Ivory Coast and French infants. *International Journal of Psychology, 25*, 337–342.

Age and ethnic group differences in visual habituation rate were investigated in three-, five-, and eight-month-old French and Ivory Coast infants. An infant-controlled procedure was used to assess visual fixation. For the French infants, the image of a white woman was projected, and for the Ivory Coast infants, the image of a black woman was projected.

319. Lerer, L., Butchart, A., & Blanche, M. (1995). "A bothersome death": Narrative accounts of infant mortality in Cape Town, South Africa. *Social Science and Medicine, 40*, 945–953.

The behavior of caregivers and health care providers was examined to determine the effect on infant mortality in Cape Town, South Africa. Verbal histories were provided by the caregivers of 70 infants in the course of obtaining police death certification. Infants with a respiratory condition were likely to have been taken for medical attention prior to death. In contrast, the parents of infants with diarrheal disease were less likely to seek medical care.

320. Lusk, D., & Lewis, M. (1972). Mother-infant interaction and infant development among the Wolof of Senegal. *Human Development, 15*, 58–69.

Patterns of early caretaker-infant interaction were examined in a sample of Wolof infants over the first year of life. Specific types of caretaker-infant behaviors were most related to the infant's age. These Wolof infants manifested precocious development during the first year, consistent with prior studies of African infants.

321. Muhudhia, S.O., & Musoke, R.N. (1989). Postnatal weight gain of exclusively breast-fed pre term African infants. *Journal of Tropical Pediatrics, 35*, 241–244.

Weights were tracked for preterm, breast-fed infants assessed as appropriate for their gestational ages while they resided in the newborn unit. The infants were classified into three groups based on BW: A (1,001–1,250 g), B (1,250–1,500 g), and C (1,501–1,750 g). All groups were observed to experience significant weight loss during the first week: A (12.0%), B (7.7%), and C (4.4%). By 23, 16, and 15 days, respectively, BW had been regained.

322. Nyirjesy, K.M., & Nyirjesy, P. (1991). Neonatal care in northeast Zaire. *Journal of Obstetric, Gynecologic, and Neonatal Nursing, 20,* 362–366.

Many challenges to neonatal care exist in rural northeast Zaire. Multiple factors contribute to the high infant mortality rate and difficulty with neonatal care, including widespread infectious disease, limited resources, poor public education, and cultural beliefs. To meet the basic needs of newborn infants for warmth, respiration, nutrition, and prevention of infection, midwives resort to innovative nursing interventions.

323. Okeahialam, T. (1984). Child abuse in Nigeria. *Child Abuse and Neglect, 8,* 69–73.

Child abuse in Nigeria has received little attention. With rapid socioeconomic and political changes altering society, various forms of child abuse have been identified, particularly in urban areas. They include abandonment of normal infants by unmarried or very poor mothers in cities, increased child labor and exploitation of children from rural areas in urban elite families, and abuse of children in urban nuclear families by caretakers.

324. Palloni, A. (1981). A review of infant mortality trends in selected underdeveloped countries: Some new estimates. *Population Studies, 35,* 100–119.

Updated infant and child mortality estimates are presented for a sample of 26 African, Asian, and Latin American countries in order to upgrade the quality of vital statistics related to morality.

325. Potgieter, S.T., & Kibel, M.A. (1992). Sleeping positions of infants in the Cape Peninsula. *South African Medical Journal, 81,* 355–357.

SIDS is related to the prone position of sleeping. Unselected Cape Peninsula infants aged six months and younger were studied to determine the frequency of various sleeping positions. Findings indicated that 62.4% slept prone with the face to the side; however, the frequency of this position varied with ethnicity (whites 50.0%; blacks 58.7%; coloureds 69.8%) and social class (higher classes 54.1%; lower classes 69.2%). Whereas 94% of black infants and 71% of coloured infants slept with their mothers, only 4% of white infants did so.

326. Richter, L.M. (1989). Household density, family size and the growth and development of black children: A cross-sectional study from infancy to middle childhood. *South African Journal of Psychology, 19,* 191–198.

A sample of 1,011 black children, aged two months to nine years, was studied to determine interrelationships between household density, number of children, and physical growth and psychological development. Overall, few important changes in the interpersonal environments of children in black townships emerged in relation to household density measures.

327. Richter, L.M., & Grieve, K.W. (1991). Home environment and cognitive development of black infants in impoverished South African families. *Infant Mental Health Journal, 12,* 88–102.

Home environment, mental and psychomotor development, growth, and SES were studied in 2- to 30-month-old urban African infants. Regardless of SES, the home environment was significantly related to infant cognitive development, suggesting that the quality of the home environment is important for infant development.

328. Retel-Laurentin, A., & Benoit, D. (1976). Infant mortality and birth intervals. *Population Studies, 30,* 279–293.

A survey of infant mortality and birth intervals was conducted in nine villages of the Bobo-Oule people in Upper Volta. Higher fetal mortality rates were related to lower fertility rates, but higher fertility rates were associated with more child mortality up to age four. Longer birth intervals appear to be a result of a high incidence of spontaneous abortions, which are more common than previously believed.

329. Saling, M., Abrams, R., & Chesler, H. (1983). A photographic survey of lateral cradling preferences in black and white women. *South African Journal of Psychology,* *13,* 135–136.

The lateral cradling biases of black and white women were investigated by reviewing photographs of women holding infants, collected from black- and white-oriented popular magazines. Both black and white women evidenced a leftward bias in cradling, suggesting that left-side cradling is a universal maternal behavior.

330. Saling, M.M. (1984). Cradling and transport of infants by South African mothers: A cross-cultural study. *Current Anthropology, 25,* 333–335.

Cradling and carrying behaviors were observed for black, Coloured, and Indian women attending well-baby clinics in South Africa with their infants. All the women cradled their infant significantly more often to the left, with dorsal-midline transport observed in 35% of black mothers. The arm position was preferred significantly more than the hip position. Mothers did not utilize the shoulder cradling position.

331. Super, C.M., Harkness, S., & LeVine, R.A. (1974). Patterns of personality in Africa: A note from the field. *Ethos, 2,* 377–381.

Eight Kipsigis infants and their mothers were observed in naturalistic interaction in their homes. The frequency of face-to-face interaction was comparable to that of American mother-infant pairs. Qualitative analysis with parents and older children in the same community also point to intense parent-child bonds.

332. Super, C.M. (1976). Environmental effects on motor development: The case of "African infant precocity." *Developmental Medicine and Child Neurology, 18,* 561–567.

Kenyan infants acquire sitting and walking skills early, and these skills are specifically taught by the caretakers and are practiced in the course of daily routines. Motor skills that are not taught or practiced emerge at rates similar to those of American children. Kenyan children from the same ethnic background but residing in a middle-class urban environment were generally intermediate in both amount of teaching/practicing and the rate of skill acquisition.

333. Tabutin, D. (1974). Infant and child mortality in north Algeria. *Population, 29,* 41–60.

After reaching a very high level at the end of the war (1960–1962), infant and child mortality dropped sharply. From 1963 to 1968, however, no clear trend is discernable, although a slight decline is apparent in urban areas. There is a high risk of death during the first month, especially in the first week of life. The relationship between fertility and infant mortality is hardly apparent except for very fertile women. It was not possible to establish that a decline in infant mortality has exerted any traceable influence on fertility.

334. Tronick, E., Morelli, G., & Ivey, P. (1992). The Efe forager infant and toddler's pattern of social relationships: Multiple and simultaneous. *Developmental Psychology, 28,* 568–577.

A study of Efe children revealed that these infants and toddlers were in constant contact with another at all times. This created a pattern of simultaneous and multiple relationships rather than a pattern of relationships that depended primarily on the mother or one other person.

PART 5
ASIA

9 DIVERSE CULTURES, DIVERGENT VIEWS

INFANTS OF ASIA

Laurie A. Van Egeren

No other continent yields the extensive cultural and ethnic diversity of Asia. Certain regions are generally thought of as "Asia," even by the geographically illiterate. Most people, when asked to identify an Asian locale, would name China, Japan, Taiwan, Hong Kong, or Korea (East Asia), or perhaps Thailand, Cambodia, Laos, Vietnam, Indonesia, the Philippines, Singapore, or Malaysia (Southeast Asia). But many people are unaware that Asia also consists of three-quarters of the former Soviet Union (Russian Asia), Israel, Jordan, Saudi Arabia, Iran, Iraq, Syria, Lebanon, and Asian Turkey (the Middle East), and India, Pakistan, Bangladesh, Afghanistan, Nepal, and Sri Lanka (the Indian subcontinent). Racially, linguistically, economically, and psychosocially, the Asian people are highly heterogeneous.

Certainly, conducting infancy research in Asia is a complicated and expensive undertaking. And for the most part, Western scientists have devoted attention to some Asian countries more than others. Why this favoritism? The reasons are unclear. Perhaps we attend primarily to countries that produce large numbers of immigrants to the United States, or it may be that political tensions in various regions deter researchers as a result of potential danger or because of discouragement from the country's government. Alternatively, governments in areas that suffer extreme privation, illness, and mortality may foster relations with Western researchers in an effort to understand and ameliorate these problems.

Whatever the reasons, research that examines native Asian samples is relatively rare; this chapter details only 42 studies that took place in 14 Asian countries. Although a broad range of Asian countries is represented, nearly a third of the studies take place in the most populous part of the Indian subcontinent (India, Pakistan, and Bangladesh). The rest are concentrated in Japan (9), Israel (7), and Malaysia (6), with the remainder scattered among China (3), Korea (2), Jordan (2), the Philippines (2), Kuwait

(1), and Thailand (1). Notably, many countries have no infancy research in Western publications, including Russian Asia, Hong Kong, and most of Southeast Asia and the Middle East.

The Meaning of "The Asian Culture"

Beyond the problem of the scarcity of research on Asian infants, the impossibility of identifying a characteristic "Asian culture" makes it difficult to draw general conclusions about the state of the Asian infant literature. When we look to the existing writings by psychologists on characteristics of non-Western Asian cultures, it is clear that some Asian countries are emphasized, and others are virtually ignored. For example, guides to multicultural issues in psychological assessment generally limit their discussions to the cultural characteristics of Asian people to East and Southeast Asians (Dana, 1993; Slonim, 1991). Certainly, a number of cultural commonalities exist in these regions. East and Southeast Asian families traditionally emphasize interdependence between individual, family, and community, thereby encouraging the subordination of individuality to the needs of the larger system. A case in point is the one-child policy of China, in which couples were officially encouraged and given strong and sometimes forceful incentives to have only one child in order to implement population control for the greater good of the country. East and Southeast Asian cultures also traditionally espouse indirect communication styles, have patriarchal families in which elders are venerated, are highly indulgent in their child rearing, and believe in spirits, fate, and the use of herbal medicines and traditional healing techniques. Particularly relevant for infancy research, traditional East and Southeast Asians perceive a child to be one year old at birth; since the child is considered one year older each New Year, a child with a January birthdate could be labeled a two-year-old the next month (Slonim, 1991)! Obviously, reliance on the family's report of the child's age can have critical implications for developmental research.

The attention of Western clinicians to East and Southeast Asians is understandable, given the large numbers of immigrants from these regions to North America and western Europe. However, the Indian subcontinent has also produced substantial immigration, and we have already seen that empirical Asian infancy studies are concentrated in the Indian subcontinent; yet information on Indian cultural characteristics is virtually omitted from the psychological literature. Although Indians share many characteristics of East and Southeast Asians, such as strong kinship networks and a patriarchal family system, the traditional caste system and the Hindu worldview is also an integral and distinctive part of their culture (Roopnarine &

Hossain, 1992). Similarly, little information is readily available to psychologists regarding cultural characteristics of Middle Eastern countries and Russian Asia, leaving the majority of Western researchers, clinicians, and others who are interested in infant issues with limited understanding of the context in which a large proportion of Asian children develop. Furthermore, even the best attempt to describe and explain any culture is subject to a great deal of individual variation and departure from what must be simplified generalizations.

TWO PATHS: DEVELOPING VS. DEVELOPED COUNTRIES

Although a single summary statement of the state of the literature on Asian infants is impossible, examination of the studies described in this volume does reveal a pronounced theme; a clear dichotomy exists between the content of studies conducted in less developed regions, including the Indian subcontinent, Southeast Asia, and poorer Middle-Eastern countries, and the types of studies conducted in more developed countries, such as Japan and Israel.

Infancy Research in Less Developed Countries

The majority of Asian countries suffer from overpopulation, poverty, poor economies, and lack of adequate medical care and educational opportunities. These problems have a significant impact on the health, development, and survival of Asian infants. Each year, approximately five million Asian infants die; this comprises about 50% of the total infant deaths in the world (Davis, 1994). According to UNICEF estimates, 40% of the world's children suffering from malnutrition are located in India, Pakistan, and Bangladesh alone (Montagu, 1992). The tremendous disparity in economic well-being across Asian countries is reflected in child mortality rates. Out of every 1,000 children under age five, 8 die in Japan, 43 die in China, and 199 die in Cambodia. In light of these facts, most infancy research in developing nations simply focuses on cataloguing the fundamental physical well-being of infants and identifying basic risk factors for infant illness and morbidity.

To illustrate, of the 31 studies conducted outside of Japan and Israel, 24 studies address issues pertaining to basic survival, such as mortality risk factors, birth weight, and feeding practices that contribute to infant health. A few studies were comparative, exploring similarities and differences between the health of infants from various Asian countries relative to each other or to infants from the United States. For example, researchers in Singapore and Malaysia have utilized the presence of multiple cultural groups to compare birth weight and growth weights of infants of Malaysian, Indian, and Chinese origin (Boo, Lye & Ong, 1994, *336;* Cheng, Chew, & Ratnam,

1972, 342). Similarly, Yip, Li, and Chong (1991, 376) examined birth weight distributions and issues related to low birth weight in samples of native Chinese, Taiwanese, and United States infants. These comparative studies have determined that systematic differences in birth weight do exist between various ethnic groups; yet it remains to be seen in what ways and to what degree these differences are detrimental to infants and, if so, whether changes in prenatal care or altering other environmental factors can ameliorate the effects.

Most studies in less developed countries, however, concentrated on factors specific to a certain group or region that contribute to higher mortality rates and poor health outcomes for infants and children. A number of risk factors appear to be common to most of the studies, including younger maternal age, more frequent births, poor sanitation, rural location, and lack of health care. Certainly these risk factors are interrelated; conditions of poverty, which are widespread in developing Asian nations, are associated with restricted access to sanitary conditions, lack of support services, and inadequate prenatal care. Asian countries share these risk factors with other regions that also have high rates of poverty, such as Central and South America and Africa.

In addition, two studies that took place in East Asia have examined a risk factor specific to female children: preference for sons. Ren (1995, 370), in a survey on infant mortality in China, concluded that the one-child policy has had a major effect on mortality rates of Chinese girl infants, as parents prefer to raise sons who will then be expected to care for their parents in old age (females are expected to care for their husband's parents). This preference for sons does not appear to be solely a policy issue, however; Korea does not have a one-child policy, but sex differences in infant feeding practices, with males more likely to be breast-fed (Nemeth & Bowling, 1985, 365), suggest that here too, boys receive more favorable treatment. Alternatively, breast-feeding may function as a protective factor for male infants, who are typically more vulnerable to ill health and mortality than females. While these two studies highlight the unique sociocultural environment of this region, the existing research does not tell us whether preference for boy children at the expense of the health and survival of girl children is prevalent across Asia or specific to the regions discussed.

Infancy Research in More Developed Countries

In contrast to the poorer countries, of the 15 studies conducted in Japan and Israel, only three examine birth weight and physical health. These three were all conducted in Israel, taking advantage of Israel's cultural mosaic to investigate ethnic influences on infant health (Grossman, Handleman & Davies, 1974, *350;* Handleman & Davies, 1975, *351;* Otremski, Livshits & Kobyliansky, 1993, *366*). The other studies focus on psychosocial themes such as attachment, mother-child interactions, and emotional development. Infants from Japan, a society as highly industrialized as the U.S. but with very different cultural attitudes, beliefs, and values, are usually studied in comparison with infants from the United States and/or western Europe to explore differences in child rearing practices and the development of affect. Otaki et al. (1986, *365*) found that Japanese and U.S. infants behaved quite similarly (including displaying cross-cultural sex differences), although maternal behaviors were found to vary by culture. In other research on maternal-infant interactions, Shand (1981, *373*) conducted a short-term longitudinal study of Japanese and U.S. maternal feeding and care behavior on early infant development; and Sagi, Van Ijzendoorn, and Koren-Karie (1991, *289*) included Japanese infants as part of their investigation of infant attachment patterns in six countries, as did Bornstein et al. (1992, *337*) in their examination of infant-directed maternal speech patterns in four countries. Furthermore, researchers have addressed larger systemic influences in Japanese infant development by assessing maternal perceptions of spousal support and attitudes toward maternal employment (Durrett et al., 1986, *346;* Engel, 1988, *349*).

Emotional development is an avenue that has been explored in two Japanese samples. In one study, Japanese and American infants whose arms were restrained showed highly similar responses; the investigators concluded that early facial displays around negative affect are a universal facet of development (Camras et al., 1992, *340*). In contrast, two- to four-month-old Japanese and white American infants receiving vaccination shots showed different patterns of behavior and physiological response, which may be a more sensitive marker of emotional regulation (Lewis, 1993, *359*). These two studies highlight a ubiquitous issue in both cross-cultural and developmental research: universal versus culture-specific influences in socioemotional development. Clearly, more research is required in this area.

Interestingly, the single Asian study that addressed child abuse was conducted in Japan, which is one of the few Asian countries (others are Hong Kong and Singapore) that implement at least some protective measures against child abuse and exploitation (Davis, 1994). Kouno and Johnson (1995, *358*) discuss a unique Japanese phenomenon in which newborns are left in coin-operated lockers, and describe implications of changing social conditions for potential child abuse. It is likely that only in a developed country such as Japan can issues such as abuse and neglect become the focus of social outrage rather than an unfortunate normative outcome of the many problems plaguing poverty-stricken regions.

In comparison to that of Japanese infants, research on Israeli infants is more sparse, but also shows significant attention to psychosocial issues, particularly mother-child relationships. Like the studies conducted in Japan, research with Israeli samples points to cultural specificity in mother-child interaction patterns (Bornstein et al., 1995, 338; Sagi et al., 1991, 289). Israel's kibbutz system, in which about 40% of the population participates, appears to provide researchers with an especially prime testing ground for hypotheses about parent-child relationships and attachment. For example, in a study of infant sleeping arrangements among kibbutzim, infants who slept with their mothers were nearly twice as likely to be classified as securely attached as infants who slept in communal arrangements (Sagi et al., 1994, 371); however, no infants were avoidantly attached, raising the question of what the construct of attachment means for kibbutzim children (Lavi, 1990).

FUTURE RESEARCH DIRECTIONS

Given the need to improve children's health outcomes and mortality rates in many Asian countries, investigators have understandably made risk-factor identification a research priority. This tactic has met with some success; a number of salient variables that increase infants' vulnerability have been detected. However, the processes by which these variables operate are less clear. Furthermore, the extensive cultural differences between countries within Asia as well as with countries on other continents beg for greater attention to psychosocial variables. Future research with Asian infants should attend to a variety of areas:

- Apart from risk factors to infant well-being, what are some of the variables that are associated with more resilient children? Research on buffering influences in the lives of Asian children is notably absent, yet might provide alternative avenues for intervention.
- How do systemic family beliefs, values, behaviors, and interactions, as well as factors associated with the larger social context (community, social policy), encourage the development and maintenance of both risk factors and buffering variables? For example, both Sri Lanka and India have experienced severe poverty and hardship. Whereas the health outcomes of the people of Sri Lanka have much improved, the same is not true of India, despite significant investments in health and education (UNICEF, 1988). What are the differing processes that enable change in one region but not in another?

- Given the tremendous burden that overpopulation has placed on many Asian countries, intervention studies directed toward birth control and family planning need to be conducted that also consider cultural attitudes and beliefs about the role of childbearing for adult development, as well as relationship dynamics that might make family planning a problematic issue for Asian women.
- As is true across the world, Western influence, including consumerism, is becoming more prevalent in Asian countries. What effects does this Westernization have on the socialization of Asian children?
- As noted previously, no infancy research is available from a number of countries, including Russia, Hong Kong, and most Middle Eastern countries. One task is to expand our knowledge base to include these countries, as well as to increase what we know about most Asian regions, which have been sparsely researched.
- Asian countries are an especially fruitful place to study the development of affect and, relatedly, early child behavior problems. For example, Japan has a strong cultural code toward internalization of emotion, which is in contrast to cultural codes of many South American countries and of the United States. Yet there is substantial variation in these codes across Asia, which warrants increased attention.
- One line of research with ethnic Asian infants living in Western countries explores the relationship between sleeping patterns and the incidence of sudden infant death syndrome (SIDS). Yet little research has examined the influence of sleep patterns on SIDS in native Asian homes.
- Other literature has suggested that infants from thirdworld countries develop gross motor skills at an earlier age than those from more industrialized nations. Quite a few studies have examined this question in African infants, and at least one South American sample has been investigated, but differential rates of motor development in various Asian cultures remain unexplored, at least in the English-language literature.

Overall, it appears that the research available to Western researchers into infants from Asian cultures is constrained by the economic hardships or isolative philosophies experienced by many of those countries. Nonetheless, Asia's cultural variety and rich history inspires countless questions about both Asian infants in their own right, as well as in comparison to Western cultures.

REFERENCES

Dana, R.H. (1993). *Multicultural assessment perspectives for professional psychology.* Needham Heights, MA: Allyn & Bacon.

Davis, L. (1994). *Children of the East.* London: Janus.

Lavi, Z. (Ed.). (1990). *Kibbutz members study kibbutz children.* New York: Greenwood Press.

Montagu, J. (Ed.). (1992). *Children at crisis point.* London: The Save the Children Fund.

Roopnarine, J.L., & Hossain, Z. (1992). Parent-child interactions in urban Indian families in New Delhi: Are they changing? In J.L. Roopnarine & D.B. Carter (Eds.). *Parent-child socialization in different cultures* (pp. 1–16). Norwood, NJ: Ablex.

Slonim, M.B. (1991). *Children, culture, and ethnicity: Evaluating and understanding the impact.* New York: Garland.

UNICEF. (1988). *The child in South Asia: Issues in development as if children mattered.* New Delhi, India: United Nations Children's Fund.

United Nations Children's Fund and United Nations Economic and Social Commission for Asia and the Pacific (1988). *Far Eastern economic review: Asia and Pacific atlas of children in national development.* Bangkok, Thailand: UNICEF East Asia and Pakistan Regional Office.

RESOURCES

335. Banik, N., Krishna, R., Mane, S., & Raj, L. (1967). A study of birth weight of Indian infants and its relationship to sex, period of gestation, maternal age, parity and socioeconomic classes. *Indian Journal of Medical Research, 55,* 1378–1386.

336. Boo, N.Y., Lye, M.S., & Ong, L.C. (1994). Intrauterine growth of liveborn Malaysian infants between gestation of 28 to 42 weeks. *Singapore Medical Journal, 35,* 163–166.

Intrauterine growth rates of Malay, Chinese, and Indian infants were compared. After 34 weeks' gestation, neonates of mothers with multiple children weighed more than neonates of first-time mothers; Indian neonates were significantly lighter than the Chinese and Malay neonates; and males were heavier than females. Above 35 and 36 weeks' gestation, head circumference and body length, respectively, were significantly influenced by ethnic origin, sex, and/or first-time motherhood.

337. Bornstein, M., Tal, J., Rahn, C., Galperin, C., Lamour, M., Oginio, M., Pecheux, M., Toda, S., Azuma, H., & Tamis-LeMonda, C. (1992). Functional analysis of the contents of maternal speech to infants of 5 and 13 months in four cultures: Argentina, France, Japan, and the United States. *Developmental Psychology, 28,* 593–603.

Mothers in all 4 countries speak to their five- or 13-month old infants in all ways studied, but the emphasis of the speech differed, which may be due to cultural differences. Mothers of the older babies spoke more than mothers of the younger babies.

338. Bornstein, M., Maital, S., Tal, J., & Baras, R. (1995). Mother and infant activity and interaction in Israel and in the United States: A comparative study. *International Journal of Behavioral Development, 18,* 63–82.

Home activities and interactions of Israeli and U.S. mothers (total $n = 55$) and their five-month-old infants were observed for infant visual and tactual exploration and vocalization, and maternal stimulation and speech. Israeli and U.S. mothers may follow culture-specific paths in striving to meet infants' needs and in achieving socialization goals.

339. Brooke, O.G., Wood, C., Butters, F. (1984). The body proportions for small-for-dates infants. *Early Human Development, 10,* 85–94.

Body proportions were examined in 514 neonates from different ethnic groups of small-for-gestation and appropriate grown infants. Results indicated that Asian infants had shorter forearms and trunks than white and black infants. Except for the ratio of head size to body weight and their ponderal indices, little difference in body proportions were observed between small-for-gestation and appropriate grown infants. No indications of relative sparing of head growth were observed.

340. Camras, L., Campos, J., Oster, H., Miyake, K., & Bradshaw, D. (1992). Japanese and American infants' responses to arm restraint. *Developmental Psychology, 28,* 578–583.

American and Japanese infants were videotaped at 5 and 13 months while an experimenter held the infants' arms until they became distressed (or for 3 minutes maximum). The tapes were coded for facial expressions and body movements that showed negative affect. Japanese and American infants differed only in their latency to the criterion for facial response at five months. No cultural differences were found in the types of or proportional distribution of facial expressions, suggesting that facial expressions of emotion are universal.

341. Chen, S.T. (1990). Growth of weight, length and crown-rump length of Malaysian infants and pre-school children. *Journal of the Singapore Paediatric Society, 32,* 65–80.

The development, physical growth, dietary, and illness patterns of 126 Malaysian children from higher-income homes were measured regularly from birth to 6 years of age. Results indicate that boys were taller and heavier than girls and that Asians were smaller with shorter legs than children of European descent.

342. Cheng, M., Chew, P., & Ratnam, S. (1972). Birth weight distribution of Singapore Chinese, Malay and Indian infants from 34 weeks' to 42 weeks' gestation. *Journal of Obstetric and Gynaecology of the British Commonwealth, 79,* 149–153.

343. Clancy, P.M. (1989). Form and function in the acquisition of Korean wh-questions. *Journal of Child Language, 16,* 323–347.

Two Korean one-year-old girls were studied over a one-year period in order to examine the order of which wh-questions (e.g., who, what, where) were produced and understood. Results revealed that discrepancies in acquisition order appeared to be associated with differences across children and caregivers in their interactive style. Consistencies in acquisition order, however, seemed to be based on universals of cognitive development.

344. Cleland, J., & Sathar, Z. (1984). The effect of birth spacing on childhood mortality in Pakistan. *Population Studies, 38,* 401–418.

Investigation of effects of birth spacing on infant and child mortality among Pakistanis indicates length of the preceding interval between live births is a major determinant of fertility. When length of preceding interval is controlled, average spacing of earlier births is unrelated to survivorship; however, length of the succeeding interval is related to survivorship in the second year of life.

345. DaVanzo, J. (1984). A household survey of child mortality determinants in Malaysia. *Population and Development Review, 10,* 307–322.

The impact of mortality determinants was studied in a sample of Malaysian babies at two to six months of age and at seven to 12 months of age. Findings show that babies born to mothers under age 19 and aged 40+ were more likely to die in the first month. The absence of modern sanitation was strongly correlated with mortality for babies who breast-fed little or not at all; however, breast-feeding reduced mortality less than previously thought.

346. Durrett, M., Richards, P., Otaki, M., Pennebaker, J., & Nyquist, L. (1986). Mother's involvement with infant and her perception of spousal support, Japan and America. *Journal of Marriage and the Family, 48,* 187–194.

The differences between Japanese and U.S. mothers' perceptions of support from their husbands, and the relationship between these perceptions and the mothers' involvement with their infants, were investigated. Significant differences were found between the two cultures; findings highlight differences in the cultural context of family life in the two societies.

347. Edmonston, B. (1983). Demographic and maternal correlates of infant and child mortality in Bangladesh. *Journal of Biosocial Science, 15,* 183–192.

The influence of maternal age on mortality risk for Bangladeshi infants and children was examined. Associations with mother's age and parity emerged, but prior birth interval appeared to be the strongest predictor of mortality risk. Part of the mortality risk of mother's age and parity apparently stems from association with shorter prior birth interval.

348. Edmonston, B. (1983). Community variations in infant and child mortality in rural Jordan. *Journal of Developing Areas, 17,* 473–489.

A study on infant and child mortality in 232 Jordanian children indicates that infant mortality was higher in rural than urban areas and was significantly related to socioeconomic conditions, mother's educational level, urban access, and the presence of health clinics with maternal-child health programs.

349. Engel, J.W. (1988). Japanese and American housewives' attitudes toward employment of women. Special Issue: Work and family: Theory, research, and applications. *Journal of Social Behavior & Personality, 3,* 363–371.

Both Japanese and American housewives believed that mothers of young children should not have outside employment, but neither group believed that they could be happy as full-time housewives. The American housewives strongly believed that women can handle both career and homemaking responsibilities. The Japanese housewives believed more strongly that a mother should not be employed when she has a school-aged or teenage child, when her husband wants her home, and when that employment has harmful effects on marriage and child development.

350. Grossman, S., Handleman, Y., & Davies, A. (1974). Birth weight in Israel, 1968–70: I. Effects of birth order and maternal origin. *Journal of Biosocial Science, 6,* 43–58.

An analysis of BW was conducted for 96% of Israeli live births. Infants of Jewish immigrants from North African countries weighed 3,356 g, followed by Christian Arabs (3,337 g), Israeli-born Jews (3,310 g), immigrants from Western Countries (3,303 g), Moslem-Arabs (3,251 g), Druze (3,244 g), and immigrants from countries of Asia (3,223 g).

351. Handleman, Y., & Davies, A. (1975). Birth weight in Israel, 1968–70: II. The effect of paternal origin. *Journal of Biosocial Science, 7,* 153–164.

Differences between the average BW by father's country of origin were tested by assuming a normal distribution. Except for Algeria, India, and Yemen, there was no significant difference in adjusted average BW by father's country of origin. Average BW appears to be determined by maternal and environmental factors; paternal factors have little effect.

352. Kabir, M. (1977). Levels and patterns of infant and child mortality in Bangladesh. *Social Biology, 24,* 158–165.

Data from three surveys were used to measure infant and child mortality levels in Bangladesh and to determine their structure. The child mortality technique is used to convert proportions dead among children ever born to women in childbearing ages into conventional life table measures of mortality. Shortcomings of present methods of measuring infant and child mortality in developing populations are discussed.

353. Kaffman, M., Elizur, E., Katz, F., Levin, N., Lichtenberg, J., Solnit, A., & Sears, R. (1977). Infants who become enuretics: A longitudinal study of 161 kibbutz children. *Monographs of the Society for Research in Child Development, 42*, 1–54.

Failure to achieve night bladder control up to age four in a sample of kibbutzborn Israli children was related to family history of enuresis, high levels of motor activity and aggressive behavior, difficulty adjusting to new situations and routines, low motivation for achievement, increased dependent behavior, and lack of aversion to urine contact and wetness. Of stress factors, only temporary separation from parents during toilet training was clearly related to increased bed-wetting. Bladder-control achievement was better in children reared by controlling-authoritative trainers than by warm-permissive types.

354. Kagan, J., Arcus, D., Snidman, N., Feng, W.Y., Hendler, J., & Greene, S. (1994). Reactivity in infants: A cross-national comparison. *Developmental Psychology, 30*, 342–345.

Reactivity levels in infants were examined in a sample of four-month-old infants from Boston, Dublin, and Beijing. Results indicated that the infants from Boston displayed higher levels of activity. The Chinese infants appeared to be significantly less vocal, active, and irritable than both the infants from America and Ireland. Results suggest that temperamental differences may exist between Asian and Caucasian infants in reaction to stimulation.

355. Knodel, J., Kamnuansilpa, P., & Chamratrithirong, A. (1982). Breastfeeding in Thailand: Data from the 1981 contraceptive prevalence survey. *Studies in Family Planning, 13*, 307–315.

Interviews with 7,038 women in Thailand examined the extent of full breastfeeding, the type of supplemental foods given infants, and the duration of postpartum amenorrhea. The results revealed that breast-feeding mothers introduced supplemental food into the child's diet at a very early age; thus the time period for full breast-feeding is quite short.

356. Kohli, K., & Al-Omaim, M. (1983). Infant and child mortality in Kuwait. *Journal of Biosocial Science, 15*, 339–348.

The current Kuwaiti infant mortality rate of 33 per 1,000 is a tremendous improvement over that of 100 per 1,000 during the 1950s. The current rate is much higher than in developed countries (20 per 1,000) but lower than in southwest Asia (110 per 1,000). From 1965 to 1979, resident aliens in Kuwait had an infant mortality rate 42% lower than that of native Kuwaitis. More than 85% of infant deaths were due to infectious and parasitic diseases, respiratory problems, and congenital malformation. The rate of child mortality for ages 1 to 4 resembles that of developed countries.

357. Kopp-Claire, B., Khoka, E.W., & Sigman, M. (1977). A comparison of sensorimotor development among infants in India and the United States. *Journal of Cross-Cultural Psychology, 4*, 435–452.

Overall results suggest similarity in sensorimotor functioning of American and Indian infants. Infants who have more gross motor exploration on varied surfaces may show appreciation for the subtleties of horizontal space earlier than infants who are carried extensively.

358. Kouno, A., & Johnson, C. (1995). Child abuse and neglect in Japan: Coin-operated-locker babies. *Child Abuse and Neglect, 19,* 25–31.

The coin-operated-locker-baby type of child abuse, unique to Japan, refers to newborns who are placed, while alive or dead, in such lockers. This practice has been decreased by specific measures. As social conditions in Japan change, the reported incidence of child abuse may increase. Recently, the city government of Osaka organized a group specifically designed to deal with the detection and protection of abused and neglected children, but the Japanese judicial administration still uses old laws for abuse cases; new laws are needed.

359. Lewis, M. (1993). Differences between Japanese infants and Caucasian American infants in behavioral and cortisol response to inoculation. *Child Development, 64,* 1722–1731.

Thirty-one Japanese and 31 Caucasian American infants aged two- to four-months were examined during and following routine inoculation for behavioral and cortical responses. Results indicated that the Japanese infants displayed a greater cortical response and the Caucasian American infants displayed a more intense initial affective response. In addition to a longer latency to quiet compared to the Japanese infants, Caucasian American infants had a greater likelihood of being in a high behavior-low cortisol group, whereas the Japanese infants were more likely to be in a low behavior-high cortisol group.

360. Manderson, L. (1984). "These are modern times": Infant feeding practice in peninsular Malaysia. *Social Science and Medicine, 18,* 47–57.

Interviews with Malaysian women suggest that the women must likely to use commercial baby foods, bottle feed exclusively, or breast-feed only for a short time are young, have only one child, reside in urban or suburban areas, have a reasonable household income, are highly educated women, and have husbands in nontraditional occupations.

361. Manwani, A., & Agarwal, K. (1973). The growth pattern of Indian infants during the first year of life. *Human Biology, 45,* 341–349.

362. Miller, J. (1993). Birth outcomes by mother's age at first birth in the Philippines. *International Family Planning Perspectives, 19,* 98–102.

This study of 2,063 Filipino newborns found that compared to later births, firstborn infants have significant disadvantages in BW length of gestation, height, weight for gestational age, and weight for height. This is particularly true for first-born infants born to women younger than 18. There are also notable health disadvantages for infants born to mothers younger than 18.

363. Miller, J. (1994). Birth order, interpregnancy interval and birth outcomes among Filipino infants. *Journal of Biosocial Science, 26,* 243–259.

Data from 2,063 Filipino newborns reveal that first births are the most disadvantaged of any birth order/interpregnancy spacing group. High-birth-order infants of mothers with short interpregnancy intervals are most at risk. However, only 2% of births have both risk factors.

364. Nemeth, R., & Bowling, J. (1985). Son preference and its effects on Korean lactation practices. *Journal of Biosocial Science, 17,* 451–459.

Data from the 1974 Korean National Fertility Survey indicates that the sex of a child influences the probability of it being breast-fed. Even for women with a living son, there are greater-than-average odds that they will not breast-feed an infant girl. The sex of the child does not, however, influence the number of months he or she is breast-fed.

365. Otaki, M., Durrett, M., Richards, P., Nyquist, L., & Pennebaker, J. (1986). Maternal and infant behavior in Japan and America. *Journal of Cross Cultural Psychology, 17,* 251–268.

Observations of 30 U.S. and 52 Japanese mother-infant dyads indicated that Japanese mothers spent more time with their babies than U.S. mothers, and U.S. mothers were more active in positioning the infants' bodies. Infant behaviors between the two cultures were strikingly similar. However, U.S. babies displayed more sucking behaviors. Across cultures, male babies were awake more and received more rocking than females.

366. Otremski, I., Livshits, G., & Kobyliansky, E. (1993). Ethnic and family factors in early human growth and morbidity in Israel. *Collegium Antropologicum, 17,* 287–295.

Ethnic factors in early childhood motor and physical development and morbidity were examined longitudinally for 1,000+ infants. Ethnicity did not contribute to the variance in developmental milestones, although gestational age and family characteristics did. Body size of infants during the first two years varied considerably by ethnicity. Infants with mixed parentage (North African and Middle Eastern) were significantly healthier than the others, and mixed-parentage babies as a group were slightly healthier than those with nonmixed parentage.

367. Petersen, S.A., & Wailoo, M.P. (1994). Interactions between infant care practices and physiological development in Asian infants. *Early Human Development, 38,* 181–186.

White babies with adultlike nighttime temperature patterns share characteristics with SIDS victims. This study determined that a small sample of Asian and white infants had similar body temperature patterns. However, the Asian babies seemed to develop the adult-like temperature pattern later than white babies. A larger portion of Asian infants slept in their parents' bed, these co-sleeping infants had higher body temperatures than the infants who slept in their own bed. Although both Asian and white infants slept under similar amounts of bedding, Asian babies slept in warmer rooms.

368. Purohit, M., Purohit, N., Saxena, S., & Mehta, J. (1977). Effect of various factors influencing physical growth of Indian infants from birth to six months. A longitudinal study. *Indian Journal of Pediatrics, 44,* 327–340.

369. Purohit, M., Purohit, N., Saxena, S., & Mehta, J. (1978). Behavioural development of Indian infants from birth to six months. *Indian Journal of Pediatrics, 45,* 168–176.

370. Ren, X. (1995). Sex differences in infant and child mortality in three provinces in China. *Social Science and Medicine, 40,* 1259–1269.

Survey reports on Chinese infant and child mortality indicate females have higher-than-expected mortality rates, suggesting that son preference may lead to discriminatory practices against females. The one-child policy of the late 1970s appears to have a strong influence on survivorship for female infants and children.

371. Sagi, A., Van-Ijzendoorn, M., Aviezer, O., Donnell, F., & Mayseless, O. (1994). Sleeping out of home in a kibbutz communal arrangement: It makes a difference for infant-mother attachment. *Child Development, 65,* 992–1004.

Compares attachment classification distributions of infant-mother dyads living in Israeli kibbutzim with two types of sleeping arrangements (communal vs. home-based) among 48 infants ages 14 to 22 months. The groups did not differ on temperament, early life events, mother-infant play interaction, quality of infants' daytime environment, or any of several maternal variables. Eighty percent of the home-based infants were securely attached to their mothers, as compared to 48% of the infants in communal sleeping arrangements. No avoidant relationships were found.

372. Saraswathi, T.S. (1992). Child survival and health and their linkages with psychosocial factors in the home and community. *Psychology and Developing Societies, 4,* 73–87.

Infants ages 0 to 36 months and their mothers were investigated to explore psychosocial factors that influence a child's health and nutritional status within the context of urban poverty. Results show that child mortality and infant morbidity were dependent on such factors as feeding practices, family composition, parental education, and immunization.

373. Shand, N. (1981). The reciprocal impact of breast-feeding and culture form on maternal behaviour and infant development. *Journal of Biosocial Science, 13,* 1–17.

Japanese and U.S. maternal behavior and infant development from birth to 3 months of age were compared in relation to infant feeding practices. Japanese and midwestern U.S. mothers were interviewed at four time points to examine factors such as alertness of mother during birth, postpartum procedures in hospital, family sleeping arrangements, and general style of maternal care. The likelihood of a critical postpartum period and its possible effects on infant behavior and development are discussed.

374. Suchindran, C., & Adlakha, A. (1984). Effect of infant mortality on subsequent fertility of women in Jordan: A life table analysis. *Journal of Biosocial Science, 16,* 219–229.

Interview data collected from married women in Jordan was used to estimate proportional hazards models of birth intervals. It was found that the influence of infant death on subsequent fertility is not uniform across all population subgroups. Child survival seems to have only minimal influence on fertility among less educated women and those at low birth orders. In contrast, the probability of a subsequent birth increases significantly after infant death among more educated women and those at higher birth orders. The impact of infant death is similar among rural and urban women.

375. Woodson, R.H., & Costa-Woodson, E. (1984). Social organization, physical environment, and infant-caretaker interaction. *Developmental Psychology, 20,* 473–476.

Twelve Chinese and 12 rural Malay families living in Malaysia were observed every 4 to 6 weeks until the infant's first birthday. For the Chinese families, the extended family interacted with the infant in a large room that contained work, cooking, and storage areas. For the Malay families, the majority of infant-caregiver interaction occurred in physically separate areas from work and cooking facilities. The differences between the Chinese and Malay families in physical and social environments paralleled differences observed in infant-caregiver interaction.

376. Yip, R., Li, Z., & Chong, W.H. (1991). Race and birth weight: The Chinese example. *Pediatrics, 87,* 688–693.

Similar BW distributions and incidence of LBW were found among Chinese infants born in China, Taiwan, and the U.S. Similar incidence of LBW with different BW distributions was found among infants born in the U.S. to two Chinese parents, to one Chinese parent and one white parent, and to two white parents. The variation in BW is greater for white infants than for Chinese infants; thus, more white infants had larger BW.

377. Yusuf, F. (1981). Fertility and infant mortality levels in Pakistan: A reassessment of the 1971 population growth survey. *Journal of Biosocial Science, 13,* 189–196.

Results of the 1971 Population Growth Survey in Pakistan were reviewed, along with unpublished data on children ever born and proportion surviving, to reassess the country's real fertility and infant mortality levels. Reanalysis of the original 17,833-household survey and the supplemental sample of 10,204 married women indicates that the proportion of children was consistently underreported. Adjusted fertility and infant mortality rates derived from these data demonstrate that only a minimal decline in both took place in the decade ending in 1971.

PART 6
AUSTRALIA AND
NEW ZEALAND

10 AUSTRALIAN AND NEW ZEALANDER INFANTS

SPARELY STUDIED IN THE LAND DOWN UNDER

Carol Barnes Johnson

The countries of Australia and New Zealand share similar ancestry, geography, language, and colonization histories. Both lands were, and continue to be, the recipients of a great number of immigrants from the United Kingdom and Europe beginning in the late eighteenth century. This influx of English-speaking settlers fundamentally changed the lives of the indigenous peoples. The Maoris of New Zealand and the Aborigines and Torres Straight Islanders of Australia have undergone much abuse, at one time threatening extinction of the Aborigines. The child population in both countries is decreasing relative to the overall population, as fertility rates and the recent number of incoming immigrants abates. The research on infants in these countries is sparse, and only eight articles surfaced in the citation data bases scanned for this volume.

Australia is a relatively wealthy country of over 17 million people (Boss, Edwards & Pittman, 1995). The indigenous peoples, the Aborigine and Toree Straight Islanders, represent only 1.6% of the population, whereas those of European decent, particularly the United Kingdom and Ireland, represent over one-half of the total population (Boss, Edwards & Pittman, 1995). In this century immigration to Australia has been high, and since World War II immigration has provided for a large percentage of the overall population growth in Australia. In 1991, 22.3% of the population was born overseas (Shu et al., 1994), a higher number than at any time since the turn of the century (Castles, 1992). In the 1990s the origin of migration has shifted from Europe to Asia. Of the immigrants to Australia in 1991–1992, 40.8% of those were from Southeast and Northeast Asia (Boss, Edwards & Pittman, 1995).

The population of children 15 years of age and younger has grown only 2% from 1972, representing a decline in the total population from 29% in 1972 to 22% in 1992 (Boss, Edwards & Pittman, 1995). There has been a decline in fertility in the country, and there has been an overall recent decline in the number of immigrants. This trend is expected to continue. In the latter half of this century, Australia has made great strides to help the condition of its children, as shown by lower infant mortality rates, increasing numbers of children receiving education, better health programs and improved nutrition. Children living in poverty constitute 5% to 10% of the population, which is much lower than the number in the United States (Adamson, 1994). However, as the society continues into the 1990s and the post-modern era, the poverty rate is increasing. The family structure is undergoing fundamental changes in Australia, similar to the changing family makeup in the United States and other industrialized countries. Women are entering the work force in increasing numbers, divorce rates are rising, and single parenthood is becoming more common; all of these factors have the potential to have an impact on the state of infants and children.

The history of treatment of the Aboriginal people by the European settlers is destructive and disturbing. As recent as 1969 in some regions the regular practice of removing Aboriginal infants from their parents was legally acceptable, if not encouraged. Aboriginal infants were often placed in institutions or foster care in the hopes of assisting in their assimilation into the white society. This practice has ended, though at one time it was official governmental policy. The consequences of these forced family breakups caused identity conflicts within the Aborigines, the repercussions of which are continuing to have its effect on the culture. The Aboriginal population is young, with over 40% of its people aged below 15 years. Fifteen percent are under the age of five years (Boss, Edwards & Pittman, 1995). As the overall Australian fertility rate continues to decline, the Aboriginal fertility rate is increasing.

Constructing generalizations from research on Australian infants is extremely difficult due to the lack of research available on this subject. Only three studies on Australian infants were found. Two of the three studies concentrate on infant breast-feeding patterns; one of these focuses on a program designed to increase breast-feeding with Vietnamese mothers (Rossiter, 1994, 382), and the second centers on the behaviors of mothers while breast-feeding (Ryan & Dent, 1984, 383). The third study examines neonatal irritability in Aboriginal and white Australians finding significant group differences between the two (Chisholm, 1981, 379). Due to the history of treatment, the Aboriginal population continues to be the most disadvantaged, and as its infant population increases, the need for research will continue to grow.

New Zealand shares with Australia the marginalization between the native peoples of the island and its European settlers. The population of 3.5

million (1996) includes those of European (80%), Maori (10%), and other Polynesian (4%) decent. The Maori people are undergoing a regrowth, and over one-half of the Maori population is under 20 years of age. British working-class settlers arrived in 1841, and the majority of those immigrating to New Zealand have continued to be from the United Kingdom and Ireland.

Five of the eight studies included in this section originate in New Zealand. Three of these studies focus on infant mortality and its causes, specifically sudden infant death syndrome (SIDS). Mitchell, Brunt and Everard (1994, 381) found evidence to suggest that sleeping in the prone position may be related to deaths attributed to SIDS, while Scragg et al., (1995, 3844) found that infants who shared their beds with smoking mothers were more likely to die from SIDS. A fourth study looks at infant abnormalities across the different ethnic groups of Australia. Binney and Geddis (1991, 378) found Pacific Islander infants to have the highest rate of abnormalities (18.3%), followed by Maori (10.1%) and European (7.3%) infants. The fifth study examines the relationship between family social background and childhood problems. In a longitudinal study examining children from birth to 11 years of age, Fergusson, Horwood, and Lawton (1990, 380) found that variations in family social background influenced the child's vulnerability to a range of childhood problems. Again, additional research is needed in all areas.

It is clear that the research on infants from Australia and New Zealand needs to be broadened in order for researchers to gain further knowledge about these infants, their care, and their development. Additionally, studies that address the rich cultural traditions of the Maori and Aborigines are required to gain a greater appreciation for the heterogeneity of Australian and New Zealand cultures.

REFERENCES

Boss, P., Edwards, S., & Pitman, S. (1995). Profile of young Australians: Facts, figures and issues. New York: Churchill Livingstone.

Castles, I. (1992). Social indicators Australia 1992. Australian Bureau of Statistics Cat. No. 41010: Canberra.

Shu, J., Khoo, S.E., Struik, A., & McKenzie, F. (1994). Australia's population trends and prospects 1993. AGPS: Canberra.

UNICEF. (1993). The Progress of Nations.

RESOURCES

378. Binney, V.M., & Geddis, D.C. (1991, March). Evaluation of the routine examination of nine month old infants. *New Zealand Medical Journal, 104,* 95–97.

Of 86% of babies born in New Zealand during the first week of June 1987, 69% were European, 16.9% Maori, 6.8% from the Pacific Islands, and 4.4% other nationalities. Abnormalities were found in 7.3% of European infants, 10.1% of the Maori infants, 18.3% of the Pacific Island infants, and 2.6% of the others.

379. Chisholm, J. (1981). Prenatal influences on Aboriginal-white Australian differences in neonatal irritability. *Ethology and Sociobiology, 2,* 67–73.

Recent Australian research has revealed significant Aboriginal-white Australian group differences in neonatal irritability. Aboriginal infants and white Australian infants were tested in a northern territorial hospital in Darwin. A positive relation between normal midpregnancy blood pressure and neonatal irritability levels argues for a more complex model of gene-environment interaction during pregnancy.

380. Fergusson, D., Horwood, L., & Lawton, J. (1990). Vulnerability to childhood problems and family social background. *Journal of Child Psychology and Psychiatry and Allied Disciplines, 31,* 1145–1160.

The relationship between social background, childhood problems, and offending was studied in a sample of 1,265 New Zealand children with data collected at birth and age 4 months, and annually until age 11 years. Results indicated that whereas variations in family social background had relatively little influence on specific problem outcomes, such factors had a relatively strong influence on the child's vulnerability to a wide range of childhood problems.

381. Mitchell, E.A., Brunt, J.M., & Everard, C. (1994). Reduction in mortality from sudden infant death syndrome in New Zealand: 1986–92. *Archives of the Diseases of Childhood, 70,* 291–294.

The National Cot Death Prevention Programme aims to reduce the prevalence of four modifiable risk factors for SIDS: infants sleeping prone, maternal smoking, lack of breast-feeding, and infants sharing a bed with another person. The aim of this study was to describe the total postneonatal and SIDS mortality in New Zealand from 1986 to 1992. The proportion of infants sleeping in a prone position decreased from 43% to less than 5%, suggesting that the prone position is causally related to SIDS.

382. Rossiter, J. (1994) The effect of a culture-specific education program to promote breast-feeding among Vietnamese women in Sydney. *International Journal of Nursing Studies, 31,* 369–379.

A language- and culture-specific education program was developed in order to promote breast-feeding among Vietnamese women. Results indicated that the program did have significant effects on attitudes, knowledge, and planned and actual behavior regarding breast-feeding. However, the effects disappeared by six months postpartum. The majority of women in both the control and experimental groups who delivered children in their own country breast-fed their infants.

383. Ryan, J., & Dent, O. (1984). An introduction to survival analysis: Factors influencing the duration of breast feeding. *Australian and New Zealand Journal of Sociology, 20,* 183–196.

Life table survival analysis is a technique for examining the effect of one or more independent variables on the time lapse between two events. Here, it is applied to data on breast-feeding behavior of mothers of newborn infants derived from records of eight clinics in the Canberra, Australia, area. The most important variable influencing this behavior was SES, with high-SES mothers persisting longer than those of low SES.

384. Scragg, R., Stewart, A.W., Mitchell, E.A., Ford, R.P., Thompson, J.M. (1995). Public health policy on bed sharing and smoking in the sudden infant death syndrome. *New Zealand Medical Journal, 108,* 218–222.

A nationwide case control study covered a region with 78% of all births in New Zealand during 1987–1990. The proportion of control infants who usually shared beds with their parents was high in Maori, Pacific Islanders, and Europeans. The majority of SIDS deaths that are attributed to bed sharing occurred among infants of smoking mothers.

385. Tonkin, S. (1975). Post-neonatal infant deaths in the Auckland Hospital Board area, 1972. *New Zealand Medical Journal, 81,* 187–190.

A study of causes of postneonatal deaths in the Auckland Hospital Board area for 1972 revealed a high rate of deaths from infection. Maori infants died from pneumonia at a rate 28 times that of European infants.

Subject Index

Numbers in the Subject Index refer to Citation number, not to page numbers.

central nervous system, 38, 126, 171
child abuse, 27, 169, 240, 245, 323, 358
child bearing, delayed first, 4
child care, 81, 82, 84, 136
child rearing, 33, 306
circumcision, 51
classism, 150
climatic conditions, 286
cocaine, 39, 79, 96, 113
coffee, 178
cognitive development, 13, 17, 35, 81, 94, 106, 120, 147, 161, 186, 354
color preference, 130
communication, 7, 8, 11, 19, 77, 83, 190
community parenting networks, 89, 183
continent
    Africa, 294–333
    Asia, 152, 193, 196, 275, 279, 297, 324, 339, 352, 355, 364, 367
    North America, 297
    South America, 208, 264
coping strategies, 74, 143
country
    Argentina, 337
    Algeria, 333
    Australia, 380, 384
    Britain. See United Kingdom
    Cambodia, 189, 191
    China, 198, 371
    Costa Rica, 264
    Egypt, 294, 307
    England. See United Kingdom
    Finland, 293
    France, 276, 337
    Germany, 289
    Guatemala, 271, 273
    Holland, 289. See also The Netherlands
    Hong Kong, 198
    India, 374
    Israel, 289, 307, 338, 350, 351, 353, 366, 374
    Ivory Coast, 318
    Japan, 289, 337, 346, 358, 365, 376
    Jordan, 348
    Kenya, 296, 331, 332
    Korea, 364
    Kuwait, 356
    Laos, 189
    Malawi, 308
    Malaysia, 189, 336, 345, 360
    Mali, 299, 300
    Mexico, 262, 265, 268, 269
    New Zealand, 382, 383, 385
    Nigeria, 304, 323
    Pakistan, 344, 380

Peru, 263
Philippines, 362, 363
Scotland, 287
Sierra Leone, 303, 310
Singapore, 342
South Africa, 295, 316, 317, 319, 325, 327, 328
Sweden, 289
Taiwan, 198
Thailand, 355
The Netherlands. See also Holland
United Kingdom, 277, 279, 282, 285, 292
United States, 289, 337, 340, 346, 349, 365, 376
    Alaska, 252
    Illinois, 53
    Tennessee, 32
    Texas, 104, 128, 141, 246
    Upper Volta, 328
    Zaire, 322, 334
    Zambia, 306
cradleboard, 244, 246, 249
cradling, 329, 330
cross-cultural research, 36, 187
culture related syndrome, 231
cultures, 19, 21, 40, 57, 90, 231, 263, 307
    barriers among, 231
    differences in, 90, 337

D
day care, 50, 130, 143, 192, 347
death, 52, 87, 196
demographic characteristics, 85, 86, 115, 227, 347
dental caries, 260
Denver Developmental Screening Test, 52, 54, 254
depression, 43, 56, 59, 60, 70, 169, 239
development, 36, 54, 120, 200, 262
    cognitive, 13, 17. 35, 81, 94, 106, 120, 147, 161, 186, 352
    delays in, 28, 317
    differences, 201, 202
    disabilities, 28
    effects, 139
    fetal, 162
    intellectual, 17, 167
    language, 19 147, 208, 226, 273, 343, 354
    measures of, 93
    motor, 5, 34, 357
    psychomotor, 11
    and retardation, 1
    sociocultural factors in, 46, 63, 124, 125, 151

and sociodemographic factors, 65, 127, 165
diabetes mellitus, 241
diarrhea, 209, 263
divorce, 139
drug addiction, 28, 172, 180, 241
drug exposed, 76, 94, 96, 164, 152

E
early intervention, 253
Early Start Project, 190
education, 83, 125, 127, 144, 190, 243
EEG asymmetry, 59
elderly, 183
emotions, 13, 314
    negative, 340
English, 278
English vernacular, 75
environmental influences, 36, 150, 332
ethnic group
    African, 174, 292, 297
        African American, 8, 19, 43, 66, 74, 80, 82–84, 87, 90, 104, 140, 143, 150, 152, 178, 181, 182, 193, 275
        fathers, 80, 82, 83, 138, 186
    Afrikaans, 316
    Australian aboriginal, 257, 281
    American Indian. See Native American
    Anglo, 120, 142, 201, 205, 230
    Baganda, 312, 314
    Bangladeshi, 278, 282, 347, 352
    blacks, 2, 3, 12–16, 18, 20, 21, 23, 25, 30–32, 33, 35, 37, 40–42, 44–46, 48, 49, 58, 62, 68, 69, 73, 80, 85, 86, 88, 91, 92, 98, 106, 109, 110, 115, 116, 119, 123, 124, 130, 131, 133, 137, 142–146, 148, 151, 153–157, 159, 161, 166–168, 170, 178–180, 182, 187, 188, 195, 199, 232, 273, 326, 330, 339. See also African American
    Brazilian, 44
    Canadian Indian, 249, 255. See also Native American
    Caucasian, 40, 74, 166, 192, 354. See also white
    Central American, 208, 271
    Chinese, 191, 192, 198, 341, 364, 370, 372, 378, 381, 382
    Chinese American, 197, 198
    Coloured, 330
    Cuban, 45, 56, 205, 207, 208
    Cuban American, 187
    Digo, 302
    Dominican, 208, 212

Dutch, 274
Efe, 334
European, 173, 286, 288
Filipino, 362, 363
Haitian, 62
Hispanic, 25, 31, 62, 74, 104, 109, 115, 119, 141, 152, 173, 180, 193, 201, 206, 207, 213–215, 228, 230, 232–237
Hopi, 246, 249
Indian, 230, 275, 340, 335, 336, 342, 357, 368–370
Mexican, 262, 265, 268, 269
Irish, 192
Japanese, 194, 340, 349, 359
Jewish, 196, 351
Kikuyu, 302
Korean, 343
Latin American, 263, 324
Latino, 176, 216
Malay, 342, 378
Manitoba Indian, 247. See also Native American
Maori, 381
Masai, 301, 302
Mayan, 264
Mexican American, 11, 48, 166, 199, 200, 216, 219, 220, 222, 225, 226, 228
Native Americans, 14, 239, 240–244, 246, 247, 250, 251, 252, 253, 255, 257–260, 297
Navajo Indian, 244, 251
Northern European, 275
Oriental, 36
Portuguese, 160
Puerto Rican, 22, 40, 98, 200, 204, 208, 211, 212, 217, 231
Turkmen, 286
Vietnamese, 191, 291, 385
West Indian, 72, 290
white, 2, 3, 8, 12–14, 25, 33, 41, 42, 69, 73, 140, 145, 152, 156, 169, 180, 191, 192, 195, 198, 225, 243, 339, 341. See also Caucasian
Wolof, 310
ethnicity, 62, 69, 219
    differences, 53

F
facial expression, 340
familial factors, 63
family, 57, 63, 74, 146, 183, 326
    extended, 89
fathers, 80, 82, 83, 138, 186, 269, 351

low birth weight, 4, 6, 9, 20, 21, 26, 42, 46, 49, 67, 72, 73, 98, 102, 107, 111, 114, 117, 119, 120, 134, 135, 145, 146, 162, 175, 186, 208, 211, 242, 269, 295, 379. *See also* birth weight, very low birth weight

M

malnutrition, 118, 207, 272, 307, 313, 315
managed care, 225
marriage, 80, 86, 194, 199, 310, 346, 349
maternal
  age, 4, 60, 66, 168, 335, 362
  alcohol consumption, 164
  anemia, 178
  attitudes, 142
  characteristics, 102, 107, 108, 129, 304
  competence, 70
  death, 9
  depression, 159
  education, 139, 264, 311, 374
  employment, 349
  ethnicity, 311
  factors, 122
  health, 67, 78, 115
  health risk, 216
  involvement, 158
  nativity, 209
  parity, 243
  perceptions, 187
  prenatal health, 78
  race, 72
  responsiveness, 28, 147
  smoking, 156
  speech, 337
  variables, 163
Medicaid, 32, 136
mental abilities, 11
mental development, 38, 168, 171
mental health, 255
mental retardation, 317
methadone, 76, 126, 127
Mexican infants, 208, 269, 273
military, 72, 144, 145
mood, 197
morbidity, 248, 252
morphology, 124
mortality, 2, 3, 6, 7, 9, 14, 20, 26, 32, 44, 47, 49, 66, 73, 87, 100, 104, 106, 122, 128, 141, 151, 153, 176, 181, 184, 198, 210, 218, 230, 269, 292, 294, 308, 323, 346, 347, 355, 376, 379
mothers, 8, 19, 45, 49, 50, 103, 143, 183, 185, 314, 329, 331, 365. *See also* maternal

teenage, 43–45, 54, 57, 60, 67, 78, 105, 112, 117, 163, 175, 234
mother-infant play, 331
mother-infant proximity, 296
mother-infant relationship, 72, 103, 308
mother-toddler dyads, 8
motor behavior, 37
motor development, 35, 36, 38, 124, 158, 164, 248, 267, 297, 311, 312, 332, 366
movement pattern, 309
multidimensional components, 71
multiple births, 303

N

narcotic addiction, 172
NCATS, 257, 261
neonatal period, 6, 39, 41, 42, 47, 51, 64, 114, 118, 134, 140, 148, 164, 176, 211, 284, 309
neurobehavioral development, 37–39, 76
newborn, 7, 51, 69, 98, 126, 153, 172, 308
NICU, 114, 115, 295
normal birth weight, 9, 41
nutrition, 79, 181, 249, 374

O

obesity, 242
observable behaviors, 10
obstetrical implications, 122
otitis media, 147
outreach health programs, 203

P

parental
  stress, 183, 194
  work demands, 84
parenting behavior, 13, 25, 43, 77, 80, 84, 112, 113, 125, 168, 183, 194, 220, 233
parent-infant observation guide, 77
parity, 335
partners, 53
perinatal period, 2, 9, 41, 65, 70
personality, 17, 33, 105
Personality Rating Scales, 17
physical development, 366
  and contact, 112, 234
  and environment, 42, 378
  and growth, 326, 368, 369
  and handicap, 316
physiological function, 124
Piaget Object Scale, 17
Piagetian tasks, 81
play, 55, 71, 99, 186, 278, 354

Author Index

Numbers in the Author Index refer to Citation number, not to page numbers.

Purohit, M., 368, 369
Purohit, N., 368, 369
Pursley, D., 102

R
Rabain-Jamin, J., 228
Rahn, C., 337
Raj, L., 335
Ramey, C.T., 1, 50, 142
Rand, C., 248
Randolph, E., 214
Rao, R.P., 143
Ratnam, S., 342
Raver, C.C., 116
Rawlings, J.S., 145
Rawlings, V.B., 145
Read, J.A., 145
Reeb, K.G., 146
Regalski, J., 270
Ren, X., 370
Rent, G., 14
Resnick, M.B., 149
Retel-Laurentin, A., 328
Reynolds, M.E., 225
Rhodes, P.H., 2, 3
Richard, C., 224, 228
Richards, P., 346, 365
Richards, T., 48
Richardson, J.C., 119
Richter, L.M., 326, 327
Rinehart, H., 102
Ritter, J., 115
Robbins, M.C., 315
Robert, J.E., 31
Robinson, T.R., 157
Roden, M., 60
Rodriguez, C., 271
Rogers, R., 230
Roghmann, K.J., 114
Rogoff, B., 266
Roland, E.J., 78
Rollings, J., 113
Roopnarine, J., 83
Rosenblith, J.F., 148
Ross, A., 34
Rossiter, J., 382
Roth, J., 149
Roush, J., 147
Routhier, J.L., 276
Rowley, D.L., 9, 150, 151, 155
Rubenstein, J.L., 138, 185
Ruiz, P., 231
Ryan, K., 121
Ryan, J., 384

S
Sabeau-Jouannet, E., 288
Sagatun-Edwards, I., 152
Sagi, A., 289, 371
Sakai, L., 84
Salazar, E., 263
Sales, B.D., 202
Saling, M., 329
Saling, M.M., 230
Sameroff, A.J., 153, 314
Sappenfield, W.M., 102
Saraswathi, T.S., 372
Sasidharan, P., 16
Sathar, Z., 344
Saylor, C.F., 152, 154
Saxena, S., 368, 369
Schieber, B., 269
Schoenbaum, S., 121
Schoendorf, K.C., 155, 156
Schroeder, M., 177
Sclafani, J.D., 35
Scott, S., 297
Scragg, R., 384
Seagull, F.N., 157
Sears, R., 353
Seegmiller, B.R., 106, 157
Segal, L.B., 158
Seideman, R.Y., 257, 258
Serdula, M.K., 195
Serunian, S.A., 160
Shand, N., 373
Shankaran, S., 97
Shapiro, B.K., 30
Sharma, A., 291
Shay, D.K., 209
Shelton, C., 60
Shelton, J.A., 242
Sherradan, M.S., 232
Shifflett, B., 152
Shinn, M., 84
Sigman, M., 357
Sikes, R.K., 47
Silverstein, A.B., 161
Simpson, P.M., 157
Singer, B., 292
Singleton, E.G., 162
Slesinger, D., 163
Smith, I.E., 37, 38, 39, 164
Smith, J.R., 173
Smith, R.T., 137
Snidman, N., 355
Sokol, A.M., 102
Sokol, R.J., 91, 92, 94, 95, 96, 97
Solnit, A., 353
Sontag, J.C., 233

Z

Zaghloul, S., 308
Zaslow, M.J., 13, 173
Zeisel, S.A., 147
Zelazo, P., 192

Zeskind, P.S., 187
Zimmer-Gembeck, M.J., 188
Zupan, J., 12
Zyzanski, S.J., 146

www.ingramcontent.com/pod-product-compliance
Ingram Content Group UK Ltd.
Pitfield, Milton Keynes, MK11 3LW, UK
UKHW020415010325
455677UK00029B/897